SPANISH REHEARSAL

An Eyewitness in Spain During the Civil War (1936–1939)

Books by Arnold Lunn

JOHN WESLEY
THE FLIGHT FROM REASON
ROMAN CONVERTS
NOW I SEE
THE GOOD GORILLA
THE THIRD DAY
AND EVER NEW
ENIGMA
DIFFICULTIES (with Ronald Knox)
IS CHRISTIANITY TRUE? (with C.E.M. Joad)
SCIENCE AND THE SUPERNATURAL (with J.B.S. Haldane)
IS THE CATHOLIC CHURCH ANTI-SOCIAL? (with G.G. Coulton)
CHRISTIAN COUNTER-ATTACK (with Garth Lean)
THE NEW MORALITY
THE CULT OF SOFTNESS

THE ALPS
ALPINE SKI-ING
A HISTORY OF SKI-ING
THE COMPLETE SKI-RUNNER
THE MOUNTAINS OF YOUTH
MOUNTAIN JUBILEE
MOUNTAINS OF MEMORY
A CENTURY OF MOUNTAINEERING
MATTERHORN CENTENARY
SWITZERLAND
SWITZERLAND AND THE ENGLISH
SWITZERLAND IN ENGLISH PROSE AND POETRY
THE SWISS AND THEIR MOUNTAINS
THE CRADLE OF SWITZERLAND
THE BERNESE OBERLAND
ZERMATT AND THE VALAIS

SPANISH REHEARSAL
COMMUNISM AND SOCIALISM
WHITHER EUROPE?

THE HARROVIANS
LOOSE ENDS
FAMILY NAME
WITHIN THE PRECINCTS OF THE PRISON

COME WHAT MAY
AND THE FLOOD CAME
UNSKILLED FOR LONG

SPANISH REHEARSAL

An Eyewitness In Spain
During The Civil War (1936–1939)

BY

ARNOLD LUNN

FOREWORD BY

William F. Buckley, Jr.

THE DEVIN-ADAIR COMPANY,
Publishers
OLD GREENWICH, CONNECTICUT

TO THE MEMORY OF
DOUGLAS JERROLD
AND
LOUIS BOLIN

Copyright © 1937 by Arnold Lunn

First published by Sheed & Ward, 1937
Copyright renewed March 11, 1965
Devin-Adair edition, October, 1974

All rights reserved

Permission to reprint material from this book must be obtained
in writing from The Devin-Adair Co.,
Old Greenwich, Conn. 06870

ISBN 0-8159-6819-1
Library of Congress Cat. No. 72-85731

The Postscript: *Afterthoughts on the Spanish War* is from the
author's autobiography, *Come What May*, copyright 1941 by
Arnold Lunn and published by Little Brown & Company.

Manufactured in the United States of America

FOREWORD

THE RESEARCH INTO the Spanish Civil War goes on. Year after year they write about it. There is apparently no end to the fascination with it, and it is not hard to see why. It was a truly modern war. It was a war that entirely engaged an entire people. It was humanly and philosophically exhausting. It was the center of world attention. And—people were nervously aware of the fact, none more so than Arnold Lunn—it was a synecdoche. A rehearsal, as Lunn suspected, though he did not correctly predict the forthcoming alignments. Nobody did, really.

This volume has the fascination of a Mathew Brady photograph of the American Civil War. Diligent and detailed though future reports have been, for instance the most celebrated one, Hugh Thomas's *Spanish Civil War,* they lack the tang of this account. It would misrepresent to say that Lunn was an eyewitness observer in the sense that a front-line soldier was. But he spent several dazzling weeks during a critical part of the war in Spain, and he brought his great gifts with him. He wrote his accounts passionately, with the secure conviction that comes of knowing history, and with the skill of a man, even then middle-aged, who had already published two dozen volumes.

Arnold Lunn was knighted in 1952 "for services to ski-ing and Anglo-Swiss relations." He might as well have been honored for his contributions to English letters. His first book, *The Harrovians*, was written shortly after he graduated from Harrow College, not many years after Winston Churchill did, and is accepted as the first "realistic" "public school exposé" of the recent genre. In the years immediately after a stint at Oxford, Lunn put his hand to his father's travel business; he proved brilliantly unsuccessful because—as he liked to reminisce—he had no trouble in traveling, but he had trouble in arranging other people's travels. It was in the course of foundering in business that he discovered a central truth about himself. All people, he says, are divided by temperament. Some are helpers, others are helpees. Arnold Lunn was born a helpee, he said, and it could never be otherwise. So he abandoned the business, and took a wife, a splendid woman and splendid helper.

In those days Lunn was a militant rationalist who took great pleasure in exercising his polemical and forensic skills to the disadvantage of men who believed in religion. One of his books, *Roman Converts*, contained a rather hostile study of Monsignor Ronald Knox which resulted in a written dialogue between the two men. It is still said by observers who remember the brilliant exchange that Lunn won the battle. But he very definitely lost the war, because the analysis of Ronald Knox got under his skin. And not much later, he accepted Christianity. Back into character, as a helpee.

In Spain Arnold Lunn exhibited the kind of indignation over the atrocities visited on innocent Christians which is taken for granted—I mean the indignation—when the victims are Jewish. This volume shows not the selective indignation—a term Lunn made famous in an essay after the Second World War—but a generic indignation, against persecution and torture of any people, in punishment for their race or their religion or their nationality. Some of the most inflamed passages in *Spanish Rehearsal* are written at the expense of languid observers of the Spanish scene who simply refused to acknowledge the existence of a bloody persecution of the Catholic Church and its votaries by the strange breed of ideologues who found themselves in charge of what the press called the loyalists. This book establishes that there was someone there—a learned Englishman of scruple—who said very bluntly what it took years to wrench out of the anfractuosities of George Orwell, Wyndham Lewis, and Arthur Koestler, admirable men whose predispositions, however, made it difficult for them to see instantly, whole and wholesomely, like Arnold Lunn.

Wm. F. Buckley, Jr.

CONTENTS
PART I

	PAGE
FOREWORD BY WILLIAM F. BUCKLEY, JR.	v
INTRODUCTION TO THE NEW EDITION	xi
PREFACE TO THE 1937 EDITION	xix

CHAPTER

I.	FROM IRUN TO BURGOS	3
II.	*CARA AL SOL*	7
III.	THE TWO ARMIES	13
IV.	SALAMANCA	16
V.	TABLE TALK AT AVILA	19
VI.	TELEPATHIC MOTORING	26
VII.	BEHIND THE LINES	32
VIII.	THE MADRID FRONT	42
IX.	TOLEDO AND THE ALCAZAR	49
X.	THE MIRACULOUS MARCH	54
XI.	THE EPIC OF THE ALCAZAR	65
XII.	TALAVERA TO SEVILLE	73
XIII.	BATTLE AGAINST CHAOS	75
XIV.	SHADOW ON SPAIN	82
XV.	GRANADA TO MALAGA	85
XVI.	MEETING IN SEVILLE	89
XVII.	JOURNEY'S END	92

CONTENTS
PART II

CHAPTER		PAGE
I.	THE USE AND ABUSE OF LABELS	99
II.	AN OUTLINE OF COMMUNIST TACTICS	106
III.	COMMUNIST PREPARATIONS IN SPAIN, 1869–1932	116
IV.	THE RED TAIL THAT WAGGED THE PINK DOG	119
V.	FOREIGN INTERVENTION	133
VI.	RED PROPAGANDA	139
VII.	THE IRRESPONSIBILITY OF THE LEFT	145
VIII.	A BRITISH VISITOR IN MADRID	151
IX.	"NOTHING LEFT TO PERSECUTE"	160
X.	THE *TE DEUM* OF THE DEAN	168
XI.	THE INCONVENIENT DEAD	172
XII.	THE SPANISH CHURCH	176
XIII.	THE CHARGES AGAINST THE RED TROOPS	187
XIV.	THE PRISONER WHO PLEADED GUILTY	196
XV.	CHARGES AGAINST NATIONALIST TROOPS	202
XVI.	"THE SAD AND BITTER PROFILE"	211
	POSTSCRIPT: AFTERTHOUGHTS ON THE SPANISH WAR	217
	ABOUT THE AUTHOR	231
	ILLUSTRATIONS: Between pages 72 and 73	

Thine eyes shall see the King in his beauty;
  they shall behold a land of far distances.

                              Isaiah 33:17

INTRODUCTION TO THE NEW EDITION

THAT THE SPANISH CIVIL WAR has not lost its interest for many readers, most of whom were not yet born at the time it was fought, is proved by the fact that books about that bitter struggle continue to be published. As most of these books support the Republicans who lost the war, I am all the more grateful to Mr. Devin Garrity of the Devin-Adair Company for republishing *Spanish Rehearsal*, first published in 1937, when the war was still being waged.

In my country a substantial minority supported the Nationalists from the first, but the majority included some conservatives who disapproved of an armed revolt against what they still believed to have been a democratically elected government. In view of the considerable support Hitler had given to the Nationalists, it was also generally assumed that, if and when war came between England and Germany, Franco would fight as an ally of Germany, while Russia would fight as England's ally. When I predicted a Russo-German alliance to partition Poland, and that Russia "would do nothing to prevent a European war which they believed would end in world revolution,"[1] I was denounced as a fanatic. But until Russia was kicked into the war by the Nazi invasion, Stalin *was* an ally of Germany. On the first of my three war-time visits to the United States I saw Communists picketing the White House in protest against Lend-Lease, but for which England would have been defeated.

The Spanish Civil War was indeed a Spanish rehearsal for Russia to transform free countries into satellites of the U.S.S.R.—an exercise that eventually succeeded in Czechoslovakia and Hungary. It failed in Spain.

As the Civil War proceeded, the Nationalists continued to gain and the Republicans to lose support, mainly owing to the objective and convincing reports of Republican outrages in the more responsible newspapers. Even in 1946, during our honeymoon with Stalin following the Nazi invasion of Russia, I defeated by a comfortable majority a motion, which the Cambridge Union had invited me to oppose in debate, that "The victory of Franco was a disaster for Europe."

From the first the Catholics were, with few exceptions, opponents of the régime in which Catholics were being brutally persecuted. Protestants were divided and it was inevitable that clerics who accepted the hospitality of the Republicans should receive the most publicity. "Orthodoxy," as the editor of a Catholic paper once remarked, "is not news," and though many Anglicans, some of whom are quoted in *Spanish Rehearsal*, were horrified by the Republicans' crimes, they received very little publicity.

I once defined a Liberal as "A man who objects to the persecution of Conservatives." My father, the late Sir Henry Lunn, was that kind of Liberal. To describe him as a supporter of the Nationalists would be less accurate than to describe him as a determined opponent of the Republicans,

---

[1] *The Catholic Times*, July 28, 1939.

guilty as he knew them to be of savagely persecuting the Church. At the annual Methodist Conference in 1937, the Methodists moved a vote of sympathy with Pastor Martin Niemöller, the Lutheran anti-Nazi, and with the persecuted Jews in Germany. My father proposed an amendment that the vote of sympathy should include persecuted Christians in Spain. The amendment was approved, and my father quoted the resolution in a letter to *The Times*, and appealed for a United Christian Front against militant atheism. To this letter Cardinal Hinsley replied at length, and expressed his sincere gratitude to the Methodists and to my father.

There was admittedly some justification for the pro-Republicans who assumed that Franco, if he won, would fight on Hitler's side in what many of us knew to be an inevitable war. But far from fighting for Hitler, General Franco came to be the recipient of Sir Winston Churchill's personal thanks, in the House of Commons, for his benevolent neutrality. When British pilots bailed out over Spain they were, of course, facing internment under the laws of war. Instead, the Infante Alfonso, in command of the Spanish Air Force, gave them a good dinner and sent them by car to Gibraltar.

An indispensable source for modern historians of the Spanish Civil War is George Orwell's *Homage to Catalonia*. Orwell began as an ardent supporter of the Republicans—"Republicans" only because they were not then Monarchists. They claimed, of course, to be *the* Spanish Government. Their partisans referred to the Nationalists as "the Rebels," as the Nationalists normally referred to the Republicans as "the Reds." From the first, the Republicans were influenced and later completely dominated by Stalinists. *Homage to Catalonia* is an invaluable source for the historian because Orwell not only fought for the Republicans, and was wounded in battle against the Nationalists, but also because he was an eyewitness of the civil war within the Civil War—the Battle of Barcelona, inadequately reported abroad, between the Stalinists and the Anti-Stalinist Radicals. Those who today still believe pro-Republican propaganda cannot afford to read *Homage to Catalonia* if they wish to preserve their illusions.

The three most influential groups in Republican Spain were the P.S.U.C., for *Partido Socialista Unificado de Cataluña*, strongly influenced and finally completely dominated by the Stalinists; the P.O.U.M., for *Partido Obrera de Unificación Marxista*, mainly recruited from dissident Communists in revolt against Stalinism, and the C.N.T., for *Confederación Nacional del Trabajo*, a federation of trade unions under the political leadership of the anarchist F.A.I., *Federación Anarquista Ibérica*.

George Orwell fought with the P.O.U.M. militia.

On May 11, 1937, *The Daily Worker*, speaking for the Stalinists, attacked the P.O.U.M. as a "Trotskyite organization working in league with the Fascists." Suiting the action to the invective, the P.S.U.C. attacked the P.O.U.M. and the C.N.T. in Barcelona: In the street battles that followed about four hundred were killed and a hundred wounded. The Stalinists won the battle of Barcelona and immediately started imprisoning members of the P.O.U.M. Orwell's description of his escape from Spain to avoid arrest is one of the most thrilling chapters in a book that is a distinguished contribution not only to historiography but to literature as such. It was his experience with the Communists in Spain that inspired his two classics of anti-Communist literature, *Animal Farm* and *1984*.

During 1944 Orwell and I often lunched together. His combination of intellectual and physical courage evoked my sincere admiration. Though he was disillusioned with Communism he always maintained that a victory for the Republicans would have been the lesser of two great evils.

"The Communists," Orwell once remarked, "had had their revolution, and consequently became Conservatives." "What is the point then," I asked, "of a revolution against Conservatives if victorious revolutionaries only develop into Conservatives?" "I'll give you my answer," said Orwell, "when next we meet." But he never did.[1]

Although his hostility to the Nationalists remained unchanged, Orwell conceded the main points in the Nationalist case, as follows:

He dismissed the popular representation of the war as a conflict between democrats and fascists: "As for the newspaper talk about this being a 'war for democracy,' it was plain eyewash."[2]

Secondly, there was the government propagandists' representation of the Republicans as anti-clericals provoked by the evils of the Church to occasional regrettable excesses, but not invincibly hostile to religion as such. In fact, the persecution of the Church was carried out with Stalinist thoroughness. Few priests other than those in hiding escaped execution. Obscene graffiti decorated the walls of most of the Churches which I entered in reconquered Spain. In one cemetery the coffin of a small child had been dug up, and these mild anti-clericals had cut off the child's head and laid its truncated body across the coffin. On this point, Orwell wrote: "Almost every church had been gutted and its images burnt." And: "During six months in Spain I saw only two undamaged churches."[3]

Lastly, the Republican propagandists had enjoyed great success in persuading the outside world that the Republican government enjoyed the support of the great majority of Spaniards. During the advance to the sea in 1937, I shared a

---

[1] My contacts with Orwell and other experiences during the war and in postwar Spain are described in my books, *Memory to Memory* and *Mountains of Memory*.

[2] George Orwell: *Homage to Catalonia*. London: Secker and Warburg; 1938, p. 244.

[3] Ibid., pp. 3, 67.

car with a correspondent whose sympathies were with the Republicans. As we entered village after village where the peasants were weeping with unrestrained relief, he said to me, "I know when people are pleased to see an advancing army." There was no maquis or guerilla warfare in reconquered Spain, as Orwell admitted. "As everyone knows, with a hostile population at your back it is impossible to keep an army in the field, without an equally large army to guard your communications, suppress sabotage etc. Obviously, therefore, there was no real popular [opposition] movement in Franco's rear."[1]

Readers who still regret the defeat of the Spanish Republican government are invited to read the testimony of George Orwell, who fought for that government.

Spanish Rehearsal is reprinted (substantially) as written in 1937. No changes in the text have been made save only the removal of certain ambiguities, and certain elucidations appropriate to the passage of time. As Hitler was supporting the Nationalists, it was in *The British Ski Year Book* that my persistent attacks on Nazism appeared. Shortly before the 1936 Olympics in Hitler's Germany, I enlisted the help of Archbishop Temple of York (later of Canterbury), in an approach to all the governing bodies for British sport that were entering competitors in the Olympic Games. The Archbishop wrote a letter in which they were invited to appeal to Hitler to bring the persecution of Jews to an end before the Games began. I was present at the Olympic Games as Manager of the British Ski Team, and as Referee of the Slalom race, which I had originated. I declined all invitations to official banquets and when invited to broadcast my impressions of the organization, I confined myself to one brief sentence: "Germans, let me tell you a little secret. There are still some people who ski for fun."

[1] Ibid., p. 91.

Two years later I broke off all ski-ing relations with the Nazis. I am, I believe, the only person of some prominence in sport to have taken such a step. I mention these facts lest the reader should be misled by the mildness of my references to the Nazis in *Spanish Rehearsal.*

"The impossibility," wrote Leslie Stephen seventy years ago, "of organizing effectual persecution is now admitted." Since then there has been an ever-increasing epidemic of savage persecution, and perhaps a decreasing horror of persecution *as such.* The condemnation of the persecution of Catholics by Catholics, or of Jews by Jews, is not necessarily evidence of anything but *esprit de corps.* In this revolting business of persecution, selective indignation is of little use.

In 1946 I was invited by the Spanish Government to give a series of lectures on ski-ing. Our British Ambassador, Sir Victor Mallet, who knew that I had been invited to lunch by the Spanish Foreign Minister, Señor Artajo, suggested that I should put in a plea for such Socialists as were still in prison, and for Protestants who, though free to practice their religion, were still subject to discrimination. I did not exactly relish the role of criticizing the Government whose hospitality I was at that moment enjoying, but I did my best. Señor Artajo the Foreign Minister, listened courteously and said, "You are a Catholic and a Conservative, but you are concerned about the grievances of Protestants and Socialists. During the Civil War, my predecessor at the Foreign Office received many British Ecclesiastics and Socialists, the guests of the then Socialist Government. Can you tell me whether any of these distinguished visitors protested against the persecution of Catholics and Conservatives?"

I did my best to convince him that Anglicans should not be judged by these particular ecclesiastics, but I am convinced today, as was my father in 1937, of the urgent necessity to create a militant and united Christian front to arrest and reverse the victorious advance of atheism in general and of communism in particular.

Arnold Lunn

Switzerland
December, 1973

PREFACE TO THE 1937 EDITION

"Je n'impose rien; je ne propose rien: j'expose," quotes Lytton Strachey in the Preface to *Eminent Victorians*, that brilliant and prejudiced book, every page of which is permeated by his Voltairean philosophy.

Every writer is biased, and the true distinction is not between the biased and the unbiased, but between those who are and those who are not aware of their own prejudices.

Every writer must pass through the customs of which his readers are the officials. Lytton Strachey attempts to smuggle contraband prejudices through the *douane*, but the candid author will open his "Revelation" bag and declare his bias.

"Have you anything to declare?"

Indeed I have.

First, there is my bulky bias against those who have murdered thousands of my fellow Christians; my bias in favour of beauty, and my prejudice against those who have already destroyed so much of Spain's artistic heritage.

My political prejudices are easy to define. I accept the Christian tradition in favour of the economy of the farm, the village and the small town, and against the megapolitan civilisation of giant cities. I dislike the tendency to transform small men working on their own land or in their own business into the employees of chain stores, and I regard collectivism as the final form of the servile state. I believe in the wide distribution and redistribution of private property.

I have no panaceas of my own to suggest. My political position is analogous to the aesthetic attitude of those who say: "I know what I like, but I don't know if it's art." I know what I like, but I don't know if it's practical politics.

For one reason or another I have never voted, but if there were an election to-morrow I should vote with enthusiasm for the National Government, partly for the positive reason that I prefer peace to war, and I believe that if the Labour Party were in power, militant pacifists would already have plunged us into a continental war of ideologies.

Before I proceed, I must make a distinction often obscured in this very subjective age, the distinction between bias in the witness box and bias in learned counsel.

A jury would properly discount the evidence of a mother if her son were charged with murder, for her truthfulness as a witness would probably be affected by her bias, but no jury discounts the arguments of a counsel because the counsel is biased in favour of the client.

Bias must be allowed for in estimating the value of evidence, but not in estimating the validity of arguments based on admitted facts. Arguments must be met with arguments. The jury will decide between the pleas of counsel, and not between their rival prejudices.

To make this distinction clear I have divided this book into two parts. In the first I record my personal impressions of a journey through war-time Spain from Irun to Algeciras. During the first part of the book I shall occupy the witness box, and the jury will make allowances for my bias in favour of Nationalist Spain. In my more sanguine moments I hope that I shall make a better impression upon the jury than the witnesses who have visited the territory under the control of the Valencia Government.

In the second part of this book I leave the witness stand. I have used the analogy of witness and counsel to clarify the situation, but the analogy is misleading, for I do not regard myself solely as a counsel briefed to present an *ex parte* statement, but as one who has tried to discover truth, and is attempting to write contemporary history. *Ex parte* statements are always unconvincing, and for this reason I welcome a form of controversy which I have helped to popularize, and which consists of the exchange of letters between exponents of different views. In the case of Spain I have done what I could to clarify my views by exposing them to the test of controversy. I tried unsuccessfully to persuade a champion of the Valencia Government to collaborate with me in a book of controversial letters. When I expressed my willingness to debate with any Communist nominated by the Communist Party of Great Britain I was informed that "the crimes of the German and Italian airmen . . . have taken the subject from the realm of debate into that of denunciation." I can well understand why the Communists should prefer denunciation to debate, for I do not envy the position of a Communist debator. He must either repudiate the official policy of Moscow or admit that he is the agent of a foreign power subsidizing revolutionary activities in this country. In the following pages I have done my best to analyse carefully the writings of those who support the Valencia Government.

I shall not try to prove that every "Red" is an assassin, or that there are no sincere idealists advocating the Valencia Government. Writings on both sides in this war represent the enemy as lacking in every human quality, and this attitude spoils one of the most vivid books written in support of the Valencia Government, *Behind the Spanish Barricades*, by John Langdon-Davies.

May I in conclusion appeal to those of my readers who are out of sympathy with my views not to label me extremist. Spaniards are flattered if you describe them as uncompromising, but Englishmen pride themselves on their ability to split the difference; many are quite satisfied with themselves merely because they maintain that in this war one side is as bad as the other.

Surely the important thing about a view is not if it is extreme, but if it is correct. No one could have been more extreme than the mother who assured Solomon that the disputed child was her own, but was prepared to surrender it rather than divide it. The mother who accepted the statesmanlike compromise that the difference and the baby should be split, lost her case and the baby.

Dr. Gregorio Marañón, a distinguished Spanish scientist and veteran Radical, expressed an extreme view when he said, "Only one thing matters: that Spain, Europe and mankind should be freed from a system of bloodshed, an institution of murder, which we accuse ourselves of having incurred."

I accept this view not because it is extreme, but because I believe it to be true. I reject the view that "Every supporter of the Valencia Government is a murderer or a crook," not because it is extreme, but because it is untrue.

I should not be a whole-hearted supporter of the Nationalists if I did not believe that they were more determined to redress the just grievances of the poor than their opponents. There would have been no war had the Popular Front, returned to power to redress these grievances, set about this work instead of attempting to suppress opposition by a reign of terror. Fortunately the situation in England and in the U.S.A. is very different. Communism is a potential rather than an actual danger, but if we do not counteract Communism while it is weak by persuasion and by social justice, the tragedy rehearsed in Spain may be played out on English or American ground.

We must not only outlive the Communists but outthink them, and know our case better than they know theirs and if this be our policy we shall never need to exploit against them their weapons of violence and hate.

PART I

1   FROM IRUN TO BURGOS

I HAD TO CHANGE twice between Avignon and Biarritz, and I was grateful for the leisurely pace of the train that carried us through the foothills of the Pyrenees. The green foreground was flecked with flowers, the hills deep in winter snow. Near Pau I caught a fleeting glimpse of the Pic du Midi d'Ossau where many years ago Claude Elliott and I spent grim hours searching for the body of a friend.

I slept that night at Biarritz and took the train next morning to Hendaye. My fellow-travellers were not encouraging. I was informed that new and severe restrictions had been put into force, and that it would be very difficult to cross the frontier. My informant added that these restrictions only applied, in practice at least, to those who were crossing the frontier into Nationalist Spain.

At Hendaye my passport was examined, and I was told to go back to Bayonne and to obtain from the British Consul a statement corroborating my claim to be a British Press Correspondent. This was depressing. During my journey to Spain I had been haunted by an unreasonable fear that I should never cross the frontier. I had my plans for getting into Spain, but fortunately no desperate measures were required.

At four o'clock on the afternoon of March 13 I crossed the famous bridge at Hendaye and found myself on the outskirts of Irún.

As I drove through Irún I was surprised to see how many houses were undamaged. Irún, according to reports, had been totally destroyed, but the total destruction of a town takes time and a great deal more ammunition than was at the disposal of either army at the beginning of this war. Though the Red incendiaries made heroic efforts to supplement the artillery, their work was often cut short by precipitate retreats.

The church near the station at Irún was undamaged, for it had been defended by the Basques against the Anarchists who tried to destroy it.

From Irún I took the train to Burgos, and arrived shortly before midnight.

There was a station bus at Burgos which my fellow-travellers and I boarded. I asked the driver to stop at the Hotel Victoria. Somebody had told me that there was a good hotel of this name at Burgos, but the driver never found it. He left me in front of a gloomy building that reminded me of decayed *apartements* in a small French town. I climbed up stone stairs to the first floor occupied by a dentist, to the second floor where a brass plate announced "Pension Majestic Palace." On the third floor I discovered the *Pension* Victoria. I opened the door and was met by the proprietor in shirt sleeves. He waved eloquent arms and shouted *"Completo."* His wife made expansive gestures to prove that every chair and sofa had been let. This was discouraging, but what was far more depressing was my discovery that the bus driver had handed me in the dark an excellent suitcase, not my own.

I looked at this bag with sick disgust, and realised that my only hope of recovering my own suitcase was to wait until its indignant owner arrived, if ever. I hoped that he would dislike my bag as cordially as I detested his.

I sat down in the passage on the strange bag, and the innkeeper fetched his daughter, a captain in the artillery, and a junior lieutenant in the infantry, who all explained not once but several times that the hotel was *completo*.

At that time I knew even less Spanish than I do to-day. In a mixture of Italian and French I did my best, without success, to explain my melancholy dilemma. The innkeeper rang up a guest alleged to be an accomplished linguist, a veritable master of the English tongue. He appeared a few seconds later in a dressing gown.

"The pension finds itself completo. No mus sleepy here."

He reinforced this statement by bending his head to the side, pillowing it in his hands, and violently blinking his eyes to indicate sleep. He did this several times, and the effect produced was not one of quiet slumber but of agitated nightmare.

"Señor mus absent himself. Señor comprend?"

Señor "comprended" all right, but he wasn't going to absent himself until his own bag was returned, so he sat with his head bowed in grief while the household chorused *"Completo"* and the interpreter reiterated the fact that the señor no mus couch hisself in this location.

A door opened, and suddenly I heard an angry splutter coming up the stairs; it increased in volume as the indignant owner of the bag I had taken approached our floor. He burst in upon us, and the momentary relief on his face when he caught sight of his bag vanished far too rapidly; he seized it and he did not say, "Thank you." The Spaniards are supposed to be a courteous race, but he said all sorts of things which I did not understand and I did not ask the interpreter to translate. When he discovered that I could not follow his theme, he put the bag down upon the floor to free his hands in order that speech might be supplemented by gesture. Even if I had been able to reply in Spanish I should have remained silent, for I have learned something in my long career as a conversationalist, and the happiness of reunion with my beloved "Revelation" suitcase helped me to endure the indictment of this very angry man.

By this time the proprietor of the Pension Victoria had abandoned all hope of getting rid of me unless he did something about finding me a room. He took me up three flights of stairs to the top floor where there were two rooms inhabited by an employee of the hotel and his wife and family. The heads of the household having very agreeably vacated their bed, left me in undisputed possession of a room hardly larger than an alcove, but scrupulously clean.

Next morning I managed to find a hotel; I stayed there two nights and had no complaint of the room or of the lounge where I spent my last night in Burgos.

Burgos is the seat of the Nationalist Government, and the overcrowded hotel was a microcosm of Nationalist Spain. Among its guests were regular officers, Carlists, Phalangists, soldiers back on leave from the front, refugees from Red Spain, an Irish priest on his way to the Irish Brigade, and sad little groups of men and women who had no news of husbands, fathers, sons or daughters in Madrid, in Barcelona and in other towns under the control of the Madrid Government.

2 CARA AL SOL

Burgos has left a mark on memory that the years will not efface. As I write I see the crowds pouring into the cathedral, the side chapels crowded for weekday Mass, and the boyish figures in khaki like those who were young in 1914 and are still young in our thoughts.

I see the women praying for the deliverance of Spain before the tomb of Cid Campeador. I hear in the Rosary responses that note of imploring sincerity one seldom hears save in moments of national peril.

I see the soldiers passing through the streets, the note of gay colour in the Phalangist crests and the red berets of the Carlists, and I hear the song of troops on the march, "Up, squadrons, and let us conquer, for the dawn is breaking. . . ." *Cara al sol.* . . . "facing the sun."

Many years ago I shivered through the long night on a glacier ledge. We had no food and no drink and never did the stars march more slowly across the roof of heaven. We sat with our eyes to the east, and then suddenly a crystal point burned on a mountain ridge; the point expanded into a rim of fire and the rim grew until the full circle of the sun soared above the mountain barrier and flooded our frozen bodies with renascent warmth. *Cara al sol* . . .

And when Mola spoke on the balcony at Burgos, Spain knew that the black night of fear was past.

They had been waiting for this, the Basques of Navarre. Rumour had travelled on mountain winds, and men stood to attention waiting for the word of deliverance, the word which should summon all that is best in Spain to fight.

When Mola appealed for volunteers, dukes and factory hands, tradesmen and peasants, stormed the recruiting offices as Englishmen had stormed them in 1914. Those who remember the cheering crowds round Buckingham Palace when England went to war can picture Burgos in July 1936. But the analogy is incomplete, for we entered that war without hate; there had been no Prussian terror in the streets of London. The England of 1914 was passing from prosperous peace into a darker time. The Burgos of July 1936 was escaping from darkness into light. *Cara al sol.* They had lived for months, these men who were to restore Christian Spain, under a reign of anarchy. They had seen the police stand by under instructions from the Government not to interfere while churches were burned and gangsters looted. They had risen, as every decent Englishman or American would rise if the Red Terror crossed the English Channel or the Atlantic.

The mood of ardent enthusiasm passed. The streets were full of rumours, rumours of a serious check before Madrid. The Burgos I saw was like London in 1915, grimly determined to see the thing through—no facile optimism, no discounting of the difficulties that confronted them, but a rock-like confidence in the certainty of victory final and complete.

Burgos is the seat of Government, an appropriate setting, for it was in Burgos that the first democratic Parliament met. In the Cortes of Burgos in 1169 the *Estado Llano* (Third Estate) were represented for the first time in history, many years before the Commons were represented in the English Parliament.

I met at Burgos a lady who was working with the Anglo-Spanish medical unit at Vitoria. She spoke enthusiastically of Miss Gabrielle Herbert who has been with the unit from the first. With the exception of this unit, and other units financed by Catholics, British ambulances have been sent exclusively to Red Spain.

Two young Englishmen who had spent some weeks in Spain, Lord St. Aldwyns and Mr. Balfour, dined with me at Burgos. We grumbled about the indifference of our countrymen to the issues of this war, and we agreed that if only the English who have lived and worked in Spain could be mobilized to go from town to town in our country telling the truth on public platforms, England might yet be persuaded that Spain is fighting our battle no less than hers.

Meanwhile we have been doped by propaganda as corrupt as it is brilliant, as cynical as it is successful. The resources behind this propaganda are unlimited, for Russia is the second greatest gold producing country in the world and the Valencia Government has control of the gold in the Madrid Banks; while the committee of Englishmen trying to counteract Red propaganda have to argue for hours whether they can afford to print, or must be content to roneograph, a letter or pamphlet contradicting Red lies.

The new propaganda in which the Communists are supremely successful is not a propaganda based on argument. On a debating platform, as I know, the champions of Red Spain make no attempt to meet a single point that their opponent makes; they just rant. Their propaganda depends partly on actual photographs and partly on word pictures. The Valencia Government floods the world with illustrated magazines. They are clever, these photographs of women and children killed in air raids; they have an immediate appeal to those who feel strongly but seldom think accurately. It is easy to feel strongly when you see a photograph of a child killed by a bomb, but you have not only to feel but to think to understand the distinction between the inevitable casualties among civilians in modern warfare and the deliberate massacre of men, women and children behind the Red lines. One corpse looks much like another, and you cannot photograph the state of mind that is prepared to soak women in petrol as a preliminary to burning them alive.

The prophets of Dialectical Materialism have discovered that dialectics are not enough. The written propaganda of the Reds relies on word pictures, not on facts; the Reds are too clever to defend a hopeless case, and are wise to concentrate on word-pictures imposed by the hypnotic effect of endless reiteration. Men, particularly Anglo-Saxons, are moved by pictures and bored by argument, and the picture imposed by the Reds is a picture of reactionary generals surrounded by obsequious priests, supported by a handful of Grandees and by legions of Italian and German mercenaries.

This caricature cannot be effaced by the written word, but the English, unmoved by impersonal arguments, have an intuition for personal truth, and an hour in the streets of Burgos or Seville should dispel forever the legend which the Reds have tried to create. If the surrealism of Red propaganda could be counteracted by the realism of inescapable fact, we should see in the long columns of volunteers a cross section of national life like our own.

Even more successful than the propaganda mosaic of an army recruited from Moors and Italians is the picture of the rich fighting for their privileges against the poor and dispossessed. Nobody denies that there were grave social evils in Spain, but it is sometimes forgotten that this war followed five years of Republican government. Bloomsbury intellectuals assured us that if only the King could be deposed the Republican dawn would herald an age of prosperity and reform. If the social evils were as black as painted, why did the Left-Wing Governments in control of Spain after the King left do nothing to redress them?

People forget that during the last century Spain has been governed mainly by Liberal Cabinets. Apart from eight years of dictatorships and an aggregate of about thirty years of Conservative Governments, Spain has been ruled by Liberals. The Spanish Liberal, however, is very different from our English ideal. There have been high-minded Liberals in Spanish politics, but they have been outnumbered by the kind of Liberal who is liberal with the property of others, and who retires with the loot when there is a change of Government. Strong words, but no stronger than those used by Lerroux, the Lloyd George of Spain, for fifty years a Radical, one of the architects of the Republic, and more than once premier of Republican Spain. He writes:

> For the nation is not the savage horde that robs, sacks, and murders on the pretext of social quality, nor is it the band of intellectuals who direct that horde and who, preferring to see the work of twenty centuries of civilization reduced to nothing, had not the courage to perish with it nor the strength of mind to shoulder the responsibilities they had incurred. Before seeking safety in flight and sure of impunity, they have robbed private treasures and pillaged the Treasury of the nation, and now leave behind them, a prey to the horrors of the battlefield, the wretched herd that has to pay with its blood.

If the Red terror, following the return of the Popular Front to power, had occurred during the reign of reactionaries, it would have been less easy to defend. The violence of the poor is sometimes the only weapon against the avarice of the rich, but a Left-Wing Government charged to redress grievances was in power, and the Opposition had pledged cooperation in this task. The gangsters of the Left, however, were less interested in social reform than in assassination, arson and loot.

The nation, not only the Army, has risen against this.

> The Army has not broken with discipline [writes Lerroux], it seeks to restore a discipline broken by anti-patriotic traitors and criminal anarchists; it has not risen against the law, but for the law, so that law and authority should rule, not against the people, but for the safety of the people. It is by no means a question of a military *pronunciamiento,* but of a national rising as legitimate and holy as the War of Independence in 1808. It is even more sacred, for it is a question not only of political independence, but of social and economic organization, of the protection of home property, culture, conscience, and very life; of a whole civilization as handed down in history.
>
> When the Army took up arms, it was already identified with the people; and the people, without distinction of class or outlook, deliberately took its stand by the side of the Army.

When Englishmen gather in Spain a note of exasperation creeps into their voices. How can people at home be so blind? Must they wait for barricades in Bond Street before they see the Red light? Let them not forget that if Russia wins in Spain, France will be the next objective, and if France falls, the Spanish war may yet be refought on English soil. The trenches round Madrid are the front line trenches of the unending war between civilization and subversive forces.

"It can't happen here." I wonder. Complacency and apathy are the breeding ground of revolution. My views are not only the result of reading. I was in Germany after the War when Communists were fighting for control, and I was in Berlin during the Communist upheavals of 1919. I have studied the effect of Communism in Italy and the methods of Communism in the United States and Canada. I have accumulated Communist propaganda literature, including literature intended only for private circulation. I know that the strength of Communism in England cannot be measured by the number of those who describe themselves as Communists. The danger is not immediate, but the uneasy truce will not last.

3 THE TWO ARMIES

A BRIEF SKETCH of the diverse elements in the opposing armies of Spain may be of use to the reader unversed in Spanish politics.

The pre-war army comprised the Regular Army, the *Tercio* or Legion, and the Moors. The Regular Army comprised a permanent *cadre* of officers and non-commissioned officers, and conscripts whose period of military service was one year. Long-service, highly paid volunteers, ninety-five per cent of whom at the outbreak of war were Spaniards, constituted the *Tercio* or Legion. The Moors served for long periods in the Spanish Moroccan Army.

The majority of the officers followed Franco. Most of the conscripts, many of whom had left their villages only because they were conscripted, followed their officers. The Legion and the Moors followed Franco to a man.

The defection of the Navy was a severe blow, and might have proved fatal to Franco's plans had the Reds been less incompetent. The Air Force had few planes at the outbreak of war, and most of these were out of date. The majority of the Air Force supported the Government. The *Guardia Civil* was a magnificent corps with a fine tradition. Many of them are fighting for the Valencia Government, but most are believed to be fighting for Franco.

The civilian organizations, now under arms in support of the Nationalist cause, include first, in order of seniority, the *Tradicionalistas,* usually known as the Carlists. The Carlists try to maintain the historic characteristics of the various regions of Spain. They hold strong views about the evils of finance-capitalism. They are Monarchists by conviction, but have an hereditary feud with the Alfonsist branch of the Bourbon dynasty.

Acción Popular support a broad programme of social justice, and defend what has been described as the organic conception of democracy. *Renovación Española*, a section of *Acción Popular,* commands small support in the nation as a whole, but makes a special appeal to the aristocracy, and, in contrast to the Carlists, wishes to see a member of King Alfonso's family on the throne.

Finally there is the *Falange Española* (Spanish Phalanx) inaccurately described as the Fascists. The Phalangists are the extreme left of the Nationalist side.

The motto of the Carlists is "For God, king and country." The motto of the Phalangists is "For country, justice and bread." Many of them are anti-clericalists, and most of them are anti-monarchial; this explains the contrast between their motto and the Carlists'.

It is far more difficult to classify the different elements in Red Spain. As in every Spanish revolution, the control has passed rapidly into the hands of the extremists, though the moderates are retained in the Cabinet for window dressing.

Two great corporations of extremists are fighting for control in Red Spain. The first is the *Unión General de Trabajadores* (General Union of Workers), familiarly known by its initials U.G.T. The second is the *Confederación Nacional del Trabajo* (National Confederation of Labor), known by its initials as the C.N.T. According to Mr. John Langdon-Davies, whose book

Behind the Spanish Barricades is a vivid description of Red Spain, "the U.G.T. believe in a socialist state, whereas the C.N.T. do not believe in any state at all; the U.G.T. follow the doctrines of Marx," and are, I must insist, Communists even when they describe themselves as Socialists for tactical purposes, "while the C.N.T. follow those of Bakunin." Michael Bakunin was the Russian founder of the Anarchist International and advocate of the stateless society. Politically the C.N.T., a federation of trade unions, was ruled by the F.A.I., for Federación Anarquista Ibérica (League of Spanish Anarchists). Finally, the P.O.U.M., for Partido Obrero de Unificación Marxista (Workers' Party for Marxist Union) was a catch-all for Marxist dissidents equally ready to shoot the Stalinists to their right as the Anarchists to their left.

A nice, friendly crowd.

There is a question of nomenclature.

I have described the supporters of Franco as "Nationalists" because their battle cry is "Viva España" and not "Viva Rusia."

The writer, Major Geoffrey McNeill-Moss, has given good reasons for describing those who support the Valencia Government as "the Reds." They fight in red shirts and wear red badges; they scrawl "Up the Reds" behind the loopholes which they defend and daub the hammer and sickle on the buildings they occupy; they go into battle shouting "Long live Russia," and regard as treasonable the cry of "Long live Spain," which throws some interesting light on the vexed problem of foreign intervention. The Reds themselves do not regard this term as derogatory, and I do not use it in an abusive sense. I have more respect for the fighting Reds than for the ineffective Pink politicians who have lost control of the revolution which they provoked.

4   SALAMANCA

I SPENT THREE NIGHTS in Burgos and waited an extra day because I had made friends with the chaplain to the Irish Brigade who held out hopes of a lift in Captain Meade's car. The car came in due course, but Captain Meade, who is adjutant to General Duffy, had filled it with spare tires and there was no place for me. I accordingly travelled by the night train to Salamanca.

I spent my last night at Burgos in the hotel lounge. I had some difficulty in deciding a point of etiquette. At what hour in the evening (or in the early morning) may one begin to treat a hotel lounge as a bedroom, remove one's boots and curl oneself up comfortably on the sofa? Spaniards go to bed late, but at 1 a.m. I decided that I was entitled to treat the other occupants of the lounge as intruders in my bedroom and to disregard them while I prepared myself for sleep.

I arrived in Salamanca in the early hours of the morning and discovered without surprise that the principal hotel was full. One day I am going to re-edit Baedeker for wartime. It is all very well classifying hotels by their bedrooms in peace time, but the wartime traveller wants to know about hotel lounges. My hotel at Burgos, rated by Baedeker as second class, had exactly the right kind of sofa to accommodate a full length sleeper; my Salamanca hotel, classified as first class by Baedeker, had no sofas at all in the lounge, only a series of entirely inadequate arm chairs. Consequently, though *de luxe*, it will sink in my future guide book into the category of "well spoken of."

After breakfast I went off in search of the Irish College to beg for a bed. I was received with the greatest hospitality by Dr. McCabe, the Vice-Rector, and spent two nights there.

The Irish College has a branch near Barcelona, and the Vice-Rector had a narrow escape at the outbreak of war. A lorry full of Anarchists passed, and one of the Anarchists saluted him with a clenched fist. The Vice-Rector naturally refused to win his safety by returning the Communist salute, but fortunately the Anarchist was a bad shot.

I shall always remember with gratitude the calm and cloistered peace of the Irish College at Salamanca. During the Napoleonic War it was occupied by French troops who removed the four panels in the lowest part of the magnificent altar piece, and to this day the Irish College is still debating whether to fill in those vacant panels or to remove them entirely. I hope they will leave them as they are.

At Salamanca I met my friend Captain Luis Bolín, head of the Nationalist Press Bureau. We had often met before at the *English Review* Luncheon Club, and it was interesting to meet again at a time when his forecasts made in the early years of the Republic had been proved correct.

Bolín had a thankless task. He had to act as intermediary between the Military Command, whose job was to win the war, and disgruntled journalists whose job was to report it.

During my journey through Spain from Irun to Algeciras, I received every possible courtesy and assistance from Captain Bolín and his colleagues, and it is certainly not their fault that the British and American people are so familiar with the rights of the Left and so ignorant of the wrongs of the Right. The restrictions the journalists complain of are imposed by the Military Command, but it is only fair to recognize that this war presents very peculiar problems in censorship.

A Spaniard who served as a war correspondent in the Great War convinced me that General Franco's staff are far more indulgent to journalists than were the French or British Generals in the Great War. This is to their credit, for they have greater temptation to remove all journalists miles from the front line. The Germans who are trying out their new anti-aircraft guns are peculiarly sensitive to the propinquity of French journalists, some of whom may have been suspected, and one of whom has been arrested, on a charge of spying on behalf of the French. Furthermore, the controversy in connection with non-intervention made the military authorities particularly sensitive to the question of Irish and Italian volunteers.

5 TABLE TALK AT AVILA

From Salamanca I proceeded by motor bus to Avila, and arrived in the evening. If this were a book about Spain rather than the Spanish War I would make some effort to pay a tribute of affection and respect to "Avila of the eighty-six towers." It was at Avila that I first met Captain Aguilera.[1] He was a retired army officer who fought with distinction in the Moroccan War. In the present war he had the responsible position of superintending the movements of the Press Correspondents and in the early stages had had an exciting time following up the advancing army. On one occasion Aguilera and a French journalist had kept the Reds at bay with rifle fire until they were rescued from a perilous predicament.

Every Press Correspondent whom I met spoke in the highest terms of Aguilera. Everybody knew that his sympathies were enlisted on the side of the journalist attempting to get a story, and that he would pull what wires he could for the Press.

In the little room where correspondents waited for the

---

[1] El Conde de Alba de Yettes.

evening bulletins I saw a familiar figure who seemed curiously unfamiliar. I thought I recognized the face, but the red beard was puzzling until Randolph Churchill set my mind at rest. The beard, he explained, was a wartime hardship.

Except for the beard Randolph had changed little.

"I wish you'd go back to Salamanca," he exclaimed, "and tell those damned people at the Press Office that they're losing this war by their idiotic censorship. The Reds have got them beat so far as publicity is concerned. They let the Press go where they like, and consequently the Press send back great human stories from the front, and that's what the public want. They don't care a damn who's right or who ought to win. A few excitable Catholics and ardent Socialists think this war matters, but for the general public it's just a lot of bloody foreigners killing one another. If only we could put across some good stories we could get some sympathy for Franco. But in Salamanca they're more interested in killing stories than in killing Reds."

"Hush, Churchill," said Captain Aguilera, "here's a bulletin coming through. Big stuff, I can tell you."

The man at the telephone took down the Bulletin from the Front, and translated it briefly for the English correspondents.

"Army of the North, Fifth Division, no news.

"Division of Soria. An attack on our position has been repulsed with great losses to the enemy.

"Army of the South. Six members of the Red Militia have surrendered with their arms.

"Army of Madrid, nothing new to report."

"There you are, gentlemen," exclaimed Aguilera, "there's romance for you. That's the big story for which Randolph has been clamouring. Use your brains, and make England ring with these dramatic deeds. Don't forget that six militia men have surrendered with all their arms."

Randolph's outspoken criticism of the Press arrangements provoked mixed feelings among his colleagues. Some of them complained that he was exploiting his name and the goodwill of the *Daily Mail* to say what he pleased, and that he knew very well that Franco would be reluctant to expel a journalist who was the son of Winston Churchill and the representative of almost the only great daily paper consistently friendly to the Nationalist cause. Randolph, on the other hand, maintained that precisely because it would be difficult to expel him, he was in a stronger position than they to voice grievances which they felt no less than he.

The first reactions of the Spanish officials to Randolph were unfavourable, but Randolph improves on acquaintance.

"I like that boy," said Aguilera. "I was against his coming here, because I knew that we couldn't kick him out if he was a nuisance; but he grows on one, and I like his great reverence for his father."

Aguilera, Randolph and I dined with an American journalist, Charles Foltz, and a representative of the French Press and his wife. Randolph held forth on the iniquitous treatment to a French journalist who had been in prison for for some weeks; no charge had been preferred against him, so Randolph said. Why was nothing done?

Foltz hinted that neither his French colleagues nor he were convinced that the Frenchman was innocent. One of the complications of this war is that Franco has to consider the susceptibilities of his allies. To the German, as I have already said, every French journalist is suspect as a possible spy entrusted with the duty of reporting on the German anti-aircraft equipment.

"Well, supposing I was arrested," said Randolph, "and thrown into prison. What would you do, Foltz?"

"The Press Correspondents here would go to Salamanca," replied Foltz, "and unless they were satisfied that there was some substance in the charge against you, they would leave Spain."

"I wonder whether you would," said Randolph.

"There's only one thing that might stop us," said Foltz. "After all, you've been pretty free with your criticisms of the authorities here, and it's possible that some of us might think that you've been asking for trouble."

"Perhaps I'm not a fair case," said Randolph. "Well, let's take another case, your American colleague at Talavera. Would you take action if *he* was arrested?"

"Sure I would," said Foltz. "He's a rival of mine. I'd do for him what he'd do for me, and what puzzles me about the Frenchman in prison at Avila is that none of his French colleagues has taken any steps in the matter."

I asked the French lady on my right her views. She shrugged her shoulders and was non-committal, convincing me, as it had convinced Foltz, that the innocence of the Frenchman in prison was not quite so certain as Randolph had assumed.

The talk turned to atrocities. Randolph quoted a remark of his father's. "The most merciful side will win in this war. Grass grows on graves; it does not grow on scaffolds."

Aguilera nodded.

"You are right. We shall win. We are the most merciful. We shoot, but we do not torture."

A few minutes later Aguilera turned to me and remarked in an aside, "There is, of course, one aspect of this business we can't expect our young friend to understand, the existence and the influence of satanic powers. But my friend Kaid Ali Gaurri," he looked towards a Moor at the next table, "he would understand."

A few days later I met a Spaniard who probably would have agreed with both Aguilera and Kaid Ali Gaurri. He was a man of fifty-five who had been educated in England, and spent much of his life there. He was in business when the war broke out, and suddenly found himself promoted to the presidency of a court martial appointed to try various cases of atrocities in a village captured by the Nationalists.

In this village, Ximena de la Frontera, the local

"capitalist" was Victoriana Pachaco, a woman of forty-five. She owned about £ 5,000 and was the richest woman in the village, but an ardent Communist. When the Reds were in power she hired workmen to dig up the bodies of buried nuns, and having made a collection of bones, she threw them one by one on to the fire on which the village priest, Father Marcelino Bayo, was burned alive on September 6, 1936.

My friend who presided over the court martial told me that he started proceedings with a strong prejudice in favour of the woman. He could not believe this story, and suspected that somebody in the village was trying to pay off old scores. There have been occasions of this kind, and some Spaniards have already been shot by Franco's army for bringing false accusations of Communist terrorism against innocent men.

"I tried to help her," said my friend, "and cross-examined the witnesses for the prosecution rather carefully. But did she help me? Not a bit. She gloried in her crime, and declared that she would do the same thing again with the greatest possible gusto. She had made something of a local reputation as a prophet of Free Love, but volunteered, rather bitterly, the information that in spite of this she died a maid. I have sometimes wondered if her failure to escape from a state voluntarily embraced by the priest whom she had helped to burn, may have set up an anti-clerical complex. There was nothing for it, as the villagers would have shot me if I had let her off (and rightly so). The country outside the village was the placed fixed for the execution, but this woman sat down in the village street when she was being led out to execution and said, 'You lazy scum. I don't see why I should help you to execute me. You can carry me to the cemetery. I won't walk.' She died shaking a clenched fist with a cry of 'Long Live Russia!' "

During dinner Randolph Churchill defined his political credo:

"I believe with passionate conviction in free speech," he

declared. "I think there's a case for denying free speech to Fascists and to Communists in England because it's part of their programme to deny free speech to their opponents, but I'd fight cheerfully to preserve the sacred right of every Englishman to hold forth in Hyde Park and to shout 'Damn Baldwin' at the top of his voice."

"And 'Damn Churchill'?" I asked.

"Certainly. 'Damn Baldwin,' 'Damn Churchill,' 'Damn Attlee,' 'Damn them all.' As long as an Englishman can damn politicians in Hyde Park, England will remain one of the few civilized spots on this mouldy planet."

"It might be more civilised," I suggested tentatively, "if the Englishman were free not only to damn Baldwin but also to damn Selfridge, Beaverbrook or whoever happened to be his boss."

"What are you driving at?" asked Randolph.

"Just this. Mussolini is the only dictator in Italy, but there are many industrial dictators in England. In Italy the workman who is sacked has the right to appeal to a Labour Court on which both workmen and employers are represented, and I am told that the majority of these appeals are decided in favour of the workman. I am sure, however, that our great industrialists would be horrified by any attempt to introduce economic democracy in England."

The problem of free speech is not so simple as Randolph Churchill seemed to imagine.

"Every man is entitled," said Samuel Johnson, "to utter what he pleases, and every other man is entitled to knock him down for it. Martyrdom is the test."

Our view is different. We believe that every man is entitled to utter what he pleases, and the police are there to see that nobody knocks him down for it. Martyrdom makes trouble.

Our attitude to free speech, like our attitude to everything else, is opportunistic. In this, as in other matters, we are guided by expediency. We do not imprison atheists because we do not think atheism matters. We imprison men who seek to sow disaffection in the army or navy because we value more highly our defences against Germany than our defences against atheism. We are not less intolerant than our ancestors, but we are intolerant about different things. A man may say roughly what he likes in Hyde Park, but in free England he is not permitted to wear a black shirt in a procession. "Damn Baldwin" is not provocative to Earl Baldwin, but a black shirt is highly provocative to those who are working for a dictatorship of the Red Shirts. We don't mind people saying what they like about the next world because we are not sure there is a next world. We strongly discourage people from saying what they like about rich people because we are certain that there is such a thing as property.

We believe in religious toleration up to a point, but only up to a point. We imprison conscientious objectors in wartime, and even in peacetime we should not be prepared to tolerate the indiscriminate propaganda of all religions. Hinduism, in which little girls act as temple prostitutes, is a case in point. If a Hindu missionary made converts in Hyde Park, and if as a result little English girls were sent out to India to serve as temple prostitutes, the apostles of Hinduism would deservedly receive short shrift.

Meanwhile, as Randolph remarked, people are free to damn whomever they please.

6 TELEPATHIC MOTORING

Captain Aguilera, in whose car I was to spend the next three days, is not only a soldier but a scholar. He would have been at home in the Greek world, for the Greeks would not have understood the distinction between intellectuals and men of action. Socrates fought with distinction as a hoplite at Potidaea, and twice saved the life of Alcibiades in battle. Aeschylus fought at Marathon, and Thucydides was a naval commander who came with seven ships to the rescue at the taking of Antipolis.

"Fancy old Hallam," comments Fitzgerald, "sticking to his gun at Martello tower. This is the way to make men write well. This is the way to make literature respectable. Oh, Alfred Tennyson, could you but have had the luck to be put to such employment!"

I was more impressed by Aguilera's driving than by his scholarship. The Spaniard is oriental in his fatalism and in his stoic indifference to death. Nobody who has been driven for a few hundred miles by a Spanish driver would dispute these facts. We left Avila in the early morning and for the first hour on the road we met nothing coming from the opposite direction. During this hour I tried in vain to discover the Spanish rule of the road. I did not like to ask, for it seemed to me that any intelligent man should be able to answer this question for himself, so I tried to guess. But as we were always on the centre of the road on the straight and invariably cornered on the inside of the curve, I did not solve this problem until we missed by inches a lorry, fortunately met not exactly at a bend, but a few yards beyond it.

On a good open road Aguilera would slow down to sixty miles an hour before turning a corner; on bad roads he would crawl round at a miserable forty miles an hour. I am not guessing. I kept my eyes on his speedometer.

"Why do you *always* corner on the inside?" I asked plaintively.

"Because at this speed," he replied, "we might skid into a ditch or over a precipice if we cornered on the outside."

"And why at this speed? Why not slow down?"

"Well, if you slow down, you lose ten seconds per corner, which means ten minutes in the day, and nearly an hour in the week."

I pointed out mildly that we had been forty-five minutes late in starting that morning, and so far as I was concerned I would prefer to regard those forty-five minutes as irrevocably lost. Life is sweet, and I made one more feeble effort for its prolongation. "Why not toot? At least you might blow your horn."

"The other chap wouldn't hear it," Aguilera said grimly, "he would be coming too fast."

The French drive fast, but Aguilera told me with a chuckle that French chauffeurs near the Spanish frontier stop their cars if they hear a car coming from the south. The car may be driven by a Spaniard.

The foreign driver in Spain soon discovers that though it is advisable to observe the rule of the road in towns and on crowded highways, it is safest to take all turns on the extreme outside of the bend.

Two Spaniards, if they happened to meet on a bend, inevitably meet on the inside; one will be legally in the right, and both will be dead.

It would be unjust to Aguilera to imply that he never blew his horn. "I had to hoot," he remarked apologetically on one occasion, "I wanted to get the sentry out of his box."

My friend Douglas Jerrold's experiences in Spain were even more unnerving. He had a driver far less expert than Captain Aguilera and considerably rasher. So much so that on one occasion his companion, Señor Merry del Val, so far forgot himself as to murmur: "If you like, you could tell the chauffeur to go a little slower."

No Spaniard could pass on so disgraceful a message, but the English, with their queer prejudice against sudden death, can do these things. A few minutes later the chauffeur, justly irritated by this reflection on his skill, cornered at sixty on a greasy road and recovered from an appalling skid to find his car all but blocked by a big cart carrying a large barrel of olive oil. The barrel of olive oil shot over Jerrold's head, missing it by inches, and the car went into the ditch. As they climbed out of the ditch the chauffeur remarked resentfully, "It would have been all right if it had not been for the barrel."

It is difficult on any reasonable theory of chances to explain the fact that Aguilera is still alive. Sooner or later, one would think, he would meet his opposite number on a corner, but he has not met him yet. I asked him if he could provide a clue to this question.

"The fact is," he said gravely, "that I have a curious kind of sixth sense. Call it clairvoyance or telepathy or what you will. I just *know* when a car is meeting me round the next bend, and I slow up and get to the other side of the road."

A terrifying remark.

On my return to England I sent him an edited copy of *You Have Been Warned*, with a contribution of my own to the famous series of "Last Words":

"I can sense a car by clairvoyance."

Franco's confidence in the clairvoyance of Spanish drivers would appear to have been shaken, for I read in Salamanca a public notice, signed by Franco, drawing attention to the ever-increasing number of motor accidents behind the line.

The thrill of Spanish motoring tends to blunt the edge of minor excitements incidental to travel near the front line. In this war the front is ill-defined, and more than one party has strayed into enemy lines with tragic results for the Spanish occupants of the straying car.

I remember emerging from a little village near the line to discover a signpost obligingly labelled "Al enemigo." Aguilera reversed, and the back wheels stuck in the ditch.

"We'd better get out of this quick," said Aguilera, "if we don't want to test the accuracy of a machine-gun barrage."

"Don't hurry on my account," I remarked. "This is the only really peaceful moment of the day."

There is, moreover, something infectious about Spanish fatalism. I have often been frightened where there was no risk of being killed, and little risk of serious injury. There is a famous slope at Mürren called "Lone Tree" and it is the ambition of every skier to take it straight. On the rare occasions when I have pointed my skis down that slope, my knees have been as wax. But Aguilera's skill, if not his clairvoyance, enabled me to enjoy those days in his car with hardly an uneasy moment.

The contrast between my composure in his car, where the risk was not inconsiderable, and my discomposure on "Lone Tree" slope, is humiliating, for it is yet another illustration of the melancholy fact that our reactions are influenced far more strongly by emotion than by reason. None the less there was a rational basis for my confidence in Aguilera.

Before we parted I had almost begun to believe in his telepathic claims, for more than once he slowed up and moved over to the right side of the road just in time to avoid a collision with a car round a bend which he might have sensed but could not have seen.

And there were more rational grounds for my faith, for his skill was uncanny. I remember one occasion when his clairvoyant talent was not functioning. We were whizzing down a mountain road with a sharp drop to our left. We had cornered, on the wrong side as usual, and as we came round the corner we met a huge lorry. This failed to disconcert Aguilera who swept out of its way with his usual adroitness. He was, however, taken completely by surprise when a big trailer attached to the lorry swung out as the lorry passed us, and almost forced us over the edge of the mountain road.

Einstein alone could explain how Aguilera contrived to render ridiculous the laws of normal time and space and to thread a swift, decisive and breath-taking course between the swinging trailer and the mountain slope below.

So it would seem that telepathy must be reinforced by relativity to explain the continued survival of Aguilera and other Spanish drivers.

In Spain it is bad form to register by thought, word or deed, the slightest bias in favour of continuing to exist. Douglas Jerrold, during his visit to the front, had to cross a road exposed to enemy fire. The Spaniards sauntered across, and Jerrold, for very shame, had to content himself with a smart amble.

I have often, in the Alps, crossed gullies liable to be swept by falling stones, and I have always crossed them as rapidly as possible. In the Alps a man who exposed himself unnecessarily to falling stones would be written down as an ass. Our attitude to danger is largely determined by convention, and I must confess that the Alpine convention seems to me far more rational than the Spanish.

I agree with the view expressed by a friend of mine whose work—as a university teacher—brings him into contact with the young. "All the better sort of undergraduate," he said to me, "need an outlet for adventure either in the air, the mountains, or the sea."

It is, however, one thing to prefer a dangerous sport to the security of mere games, and quite another matter to pretend that one would just as soon be hit by falling stones or bullets as not. The art of war consists in killing, and not in being killed. A good soldier does not expose himself unnecessarily to risks without some compensating advantage to his side. Mountaineering has its dangers; one is justified in attempting a dangerous mountain provided he does his best to reduce avoidable risks to a minimum.

Now, as a Rationalist, I can understand that the risks of dangerous driving are a small price to pay for the thrill of cornering at sixty miles an hour, but I find it less easy to understand the stoic acceptance of these risks by Spanish passengers who get none of the fun of "dominating matter, and mastering it, and forcing it to do one's will."

The quotation is from Aguilera, and the remark was made after missing a lorry by inches.

I didn't mind Aguilera dominating inanimate matter, but it wasn't quite clear to me what fun the animate matter beside him in the car was getting out of this particular sport. Aguilera has done a little ski-ing, and I have invited him to join me in Mürren after the war.

I should like to enter him for the Scaramanga Cup, a race in which two skiers are roped together. In bygone days I won this cup, and even to-day I think I could make Aguilera, a novice on skis, pretty miserable if he were tied to me at the other end of the rope. It would be my turn to talk about the joy of dominating matter, but I doubt if his Spanish pride would ever allow him to murmur "Go slow."

7 BEHIND THE LINES

On the first of those unforgettable days that I spent with Aguilera near the front, we left Avila in the early morning and drove towards the snow-dusted Sierra de Gredos.

I have spent many years of my life among the mountain ranges of many lands, and my mind instinctively searches for resemblance rather than for points of contrast, but in Spain, it was the point of contrast rather than the resemblance that impressed me.

The vertical is the keynote of Alpine majesty, but among the mountains of central Spain the driving sweep of rounded slopes serves to emphasize long vistas of roads which march with the precision of Roman legions across the plains conquered by Rome to the hills that the Romans crossed.

We stopped the car at the summit of our first pass.

Never have I seen hills richer in contrasts of light and colour. Clouds sometimes divide vertically as a curtain divides, and sometimes horizontally, the movement beginning from below as when a blind is rolled up, so that you feel as if you were looking out from a darkened room through a narrow slit to the sunlit space beyond.

And it was effects such as these that we saw from our pass. Nothing could have been more invincibly solid than the black screen of cloud slowly lifting itself from the earth; nothing more unsubstantial than the immensities of sky gleaming below the ragged horizontal rim of rain-blackened mist; placid pools of unfathomable blue showed through the dispute of storm and sun.

There was every contrast that the eye could demand. Gleaming mountain crests where sulky winter refused the gracious advances of the spring, rose snow-dusted but dark out of the middle slopes. Sunrays slanting through mists foiled their shadow with silver. The intangible green of the plains seemed transparent against the opaque browns of frost-killed grass on the hills just released from snow. The contrasts were not confined to colour and light, for the silence of the hills was shot with music, the first whispering of the streams as the sun restored to them their vocation of sound.

"The Reds," said Aguilera, as we resumed our journey, "are always ranting about the illiteracy in Spain, but if they'd spend a few months living among the mountains they might begin to understand that the people who can't read are often wiser than the people who can. Wisdom isn't the same thing as education. I have shepherds on my farms who are immensely wise, perhaps because they read the stars and the fields, and perhaps because they don't read newspapers. They have time to think about ultimate things. The long distances of our Spanish hills breed philosophers."

A verse from Isaiah came back to me. "Thine eyes shall see the King in his beauty. They shall behold a land of far distances."

Our first objective was Robledo, a little village near the front. Aguilera's son was fighting among the mountains just above the village. We stopped for a few minutes at the battalion headquarters, and a telephone message was sent to the front line to inform Aguilera's son of his arrival. As we climbed back into the car Aguilera remarked, "We'll have to hurry over the next bit as we are within the range of the machine-guns."

Aguilera's idea of "hurrying" is more alarming than the risk of a spent bullet. Fortunately the gradient was steep, and our security was therefore increased by the extra time spent in the alleged danger area. After parking the car just under the protection of the station wall, we wandered off for a stroll.

Seldom have I known a more perfect spring morning among the hills. Even winter's snow on the crests bore witness to the resurrection of colour, for the sun was insinuating colour and light and the snow was not dead like the snows of January but alive with spring.

It was impossible to believe that there were trenches on the crests of the hills just above. War and death had never seemed more remote. But the war came down to us from the mountains in the form of a handsome young Franco-Norman in a muddy trench coat. The troops, he told us, had suffered terribly from the cold. Two men had just deserted not, so their friends believed, because they had Red sympathies, but because they were almost dead with cold, and could not resist the lure of shelter.

Aguilera said good-bye to his son and climbed back into the car.

"There's all the difference in the world," he said, "between a civil war and an ordinary war. One of the difficulties of civil war is that both armies include a proportion of men whose sympathies are on the other side. Fortunately I don't think we've many Reds in our own front lines, and those we have fight like the rest. The Spaniard is such a born fighter that if you put him into a trench he will fight even if he wants the other side to win. The moment they start to attack, he gets angry. 'Damn it,' he says, 'these fellows think they can drive me out of this trench, but by God, I'll show them.'"

Heroic deeds have been performed in this war by those

who have been forced to fight against their friends. There is, for instance, the story of the officer who was in Madrid when the war started. He was sent to Toledo and put in charge of a big gun with instructions to shell the centre of the Alcázar. None of his shells fell where they should. Usually they missed the Alcázar altogether, and when they registered a hit it was always on some unimportant point.

The artillery officer was shot by the Reds. He died happy in the thought that he had done them more disservice by fighting in their ranks than by refusing to fight. A true hero, for he had risked honour, dearer to a Spaniard than life, and he had no reason to hope that his friends would ever know why he was serving with the Government troops.

Most of the Reds escape with the Red forces as Franco advances. Those of us who have visited Nationalist Spain have been impressed by the friendliness of the people. I remember only one incident which suggested hostility. A young man deliberately waited in the middle of the road and ignored one of the few toots of Aguilera's horn. He jumped for safety when he discovered that Aguilera was prepared to humour him if he was anxious to be run over.

"A fellow did that to me the other day," said Aguilera. "He waited just too long, but luckily for him my brakes are good. While he was recovering from the shock of being missed by inches, I jumped out, seized him by the scruff of the neck and bundled him into the car. The village was near the top of the mountain pass, and I drove him downhill for eight miles while he whimpered beside me. I then turned him out of the car, and left him to walk home. I bet he sweated before he got there. That chap was a typical Iberian. You know your *Don Quixote*, don't you? Well, Quixote is the conquering Franco-Norman type, tall, fair, blue eyes, and so on. Sancho Panza, on the other hand, is a sturdy, thick-set Iberian. There was nothing wrong with the Sancho Panzas until the Reds got hold of them, but of course they'll never produce leaders."

Perhaps not, but the undisputed rule of the Franco-Norman stock is a thing of the past in Spain. If Franco wins, Sancho Panza is going to have his share in running the country, but God help him if Moscow wins.

Aguilera himself is Franco-Norman in appearance and breeding and in philosophy, and his explanation of our modern difficulties is characteristically Franco-Norman.

We lunched in a little village above the valley of the Tagus. A group of women in the street started talking to Aguilera as he filled up with petrol, and this is the story that they told him:

Before the Nationalists arrived, and when the Reds were in control, the village Reds had massacred every man in the village not in sympathy with their views. When the Reds retreated from the village those responsible for this massacre left with them. Their wives accompanied them and were subsequently billeted in an outlying part of the University City of Madrid. When this part of the city fell into Franco's hands, these women were asked where they came from, and plans were made to repatriate them. They screamed their terrified protests. "If you send us back home we shall be murdered." They were right. Those women whose husbands had been murdered were waiting for the wives of their assassins to return.

One does not need to spend many weeks in Nationalist Spain to marvel, not that there have been reprisals, but that Franco has been so successful in keeping these reprisals within limits, and in substituting courts martial for lynch law.

"It is the melancholy duty of our generation," said Aguilera, "to act as the ministers of exemplary justice. We can only save Spain from a repetition of these horrors if we impress upon the minds of those of this generation a fact of supreme importance, the fact that there is a God in heaven and justice on earth."

"Have you ever noticed," said Aguilera, as we resumed our journey, "that England has always been on the side of revolution. You backed revolution in Spain, in Greece, in Hungary, in Italy and in the South American Republics. Even in the case of France the Whigs and the intellectuals sympathized with subversive forces."

Broadly speaking Aguilera was right. Wordsworth wrote one of his finest sonnets to a mulatto revolutionary who distinguished himself during his brief period of power in Haiti by brutalities as horrible as those of Red Spain. And it was to this scoundrel, Toussaint de l'Ouverture, that Wordsworth wrote:

> Thou hast left behind
> Powers that will work for thee;
> Air, earth, and skies;
> There's not a breathing of the common wind
> That will forget thee; thou hast great allies.
> Thy friends are exultations, agonies,
> And love, and man's unconquerable mind.

Selfishness and corruption in high places are the causes of most revolutions, and those who rebel under the provocation of just grievances have a right to count on the sympathy of generous-hearted men. Unfortunately, demagogues who merely substitute themselves for other tyrants to destroy all that is noble in Christian civilization, find it equally easy to exploit for their own evil ends the just indignation of the poor, and the sympathy of poets.

"Yes," said Aguilera, "the enemies of our European civilization have always found, and are still finding, their strongest allies in your country. Isn't it odd that we still like English people as individuals? We dislike your policy, your smugness and your determination to treat as a joke the character you have so justly earned, *perfide Albion*, but we still like Englishmen."

"And because we like you," said Aguilera, "we try not to be unduly irritated by your ignorance of Europe, your provincialism and your complacency."

A few weeks later I met a Spanish diplomatist who suggested that the strength of England was principally due to our immense complacency. "I remember," he continued, "a British ambassador remarking to me at a state ball under the Monarchy, that he did not think that they could have put up a better show in London. That made the evening for me."

In the matter of pride the Englishman has, as my diplomatic friend pointed out, one immense advantage over the rest of the world. He is intensely proud of his country, and so is the Spaniard. The untravelled Englishman despises the Spaniard, and the untravelled Spaniard despises the Englishman. But whereas the Englishman believes that he is the object of envy to the Spaniard, the Spaniard knows that he is not the object of envy to the Englishman. It is there that the Englishman scores. Our complacency is unaffected by the slightest suspicion that other people are equally complacent about their own countries.

There is nothing new in the self-confidence of the English. "The English are great lovers of themselves," wrote a shrewd Venetian ambassador in 1498, "and of everything belonging to them; they think there are no other men than themselves and no other world but England: and whenever they see a handsome foreigner, they say that he 'looks like an Englishman' and that 'it is a great pity that he should not be an Englishman,' and when they partake of any delicacy with a foreigner, they ask him 'whether such a thing is made in their country,' and they would sooner give five or six ducats to provide an entertainment for a person than a groat to assist him in any distress. . . . Of the English, few except the clergy are addicted to the study of letters."

Aguilera made some remark about the Anglican deans who had just returned from their visit to Madrid. I tried to turn the conversation, for as an Englishman I felt ashamed of this deputation. I remembered that though England may, as Aguilera insists, have invariably sympathized with revolution on the Continent, the England of to-day compares in one respect very badly with the England of the eighteenth century. The Whigs sympathized with the French Revolutionaries, but the persecution of the French priesthood in France provoked widespread sympathy in Protestant England. England was then as anti-Catholic as England is to-day, but no Anglican deans travelled round France at the expense of Robespierre. No less than 8,000 French priests sought the hospitality of Protestant England, and the King's house at Winchester gave shelter to 1,000 priests. For many years a large sum of money was voted for their relief by Parliament and supplemented by voluntary subscription.

We passed a group of Moors.

"The Moors," said Aguilera, "have a natural kinship with the Spaniard, for there is a good deal of Moorish blood in Spain, and we are both products of a fighting stock. We are proud to fight side by side with them, and they are proud to fight with us. After the Moroccan War we sent soldiers to govern them, and had no trouble until the Spanish Republic started sending politicians. If that had lasted we should have lost Morocco. By the way," he added, "I wish you'd tell me why it was right for the English and French to fight side by side with Sikhs, Pathans and Senegalese in the European War, and wrong for the Spaniards to fight side by side with the Moors?

I don't know the answer to this question.

Nor apparently do those who heckle me on this subject when I lecture on Spain either in this country or in the United States. Communists who are so disedified by the alliance between Spaniards and Moors, are eloquent on the inequity of the colour bar in America. Moscow, indeed, is seeking to persuade the American black man that Communism is the enemy of all racial distinctions. Nobody is more anxious than the American Communist to break down the barriers of marriage between blacks and whites.

"How can you pretend," I have often been asked, "that Franco is fighting for Christian civilization when he has enlisted the support of non-Christian Moors?"

A foolish question. A vicar whose church was on fire would not insist that the fire brigade should be composed exclusively of devout Christians. Many Christians, unfortunately, are ready to work in alliance with atheistic Communists in spite of the fundamental disagreement about first principles. Why should not the Spanish Catholic and the Moor, both of whom believe in God, fight side by side against militant atheism?

From the Moors the talk turned by a natural transition to the Moroccan War, and Aguilera reminisced about that campaign. "It's an illusion to suppose," he said, "that professional soldiers are anxious for war. There's hardly a man on either side in this war who isn't longing for peace. None the less, war has its good side. There is something very exhilarating in those moments when you have counted your life as lost and never expect to see the sun set. It is the reaction after the fight rather than the fight which is the real reward of the soldier. If for hour after hour you have seen men fall at your side and yet emerge against all hope unscathed, you experience an ecstatic exultation. We call it *alegría del superviviente,* the joy of the survivor."

At that moment we met a car round a corner and Aguilera performed his usual miracle, and I was glad to feel that even miserable civilians have their moments of ecstasy, moments when they too experience the *alegría del superviviente.*

Meanwhile we were nearing our journey's end, and the weather again was changing for the worse. Ragged ribs of thunder rumbled in the hillcrests to our right.

The last five miles of road into Talavera runs beside the river, and on the other side of the river were low lying hills held by the Reds. One of the peculiarities of this war is that the enemy is treated with contempt. In Flanders and in France a road running parallel with the enemy lines at an average distance of a mile or two was seldom crowded, at least by day, but in Spain everybody acts on the assumption that he won't be shelled until he is. Even so it is difficult to understand the failure of the Reds to cut this main road from Merida to Madrid, the principal channel for all supplies and reinforcements. Talavera is a key point, and yet apart from the river, has no effective defence. I spent three nights in Talavera, and seldom saw any soldiers in the streets. For all practical purposes Talavera was an open town. It has been bombarded from the air several times, but only once has it been seriously attacked. The story is worth telling.

At that time an air squadron, since moved, was stationed near Talavera. Its commander observed on his own aerial reconnaissances that big guns were being massed behind a hill just across the river. He was insistent in his warnings to G.H.Q., and assured them that an attack was imminent, but his warnings were ignored. Then one morning the Red aeroplanes came over just as the squadron were at breakfast. They dived into their dugouts, but their commandant was sufficiently alert to note that the explosions suddenly changed in quality. The aerial bombardment was giving place to an artillery bombardment in preparation for infantry attack. He leapt out of his dugout, and bundled his officers into their planes. They took off from the aerodrome under heavy shell fire just as three battalions of Reds came across the river, bombed those Reds and machine-gunned them until they broke and fled. This is perhaps the only time when a big infantry attack has been successfully beaten off by aeroplanes alone.

8 THE MADRID FRONT

AFTER RETIRING from the army Aguilera devoted himself to research, and he had just completed revising the manuscript of a long treatise on Spanish legislation and its influence on Spanish history when the war broke out.

"I had three thousand books in my library in Madrid," he said, "but I am told they have all been destroyed. I buy books to use them, and every one of those books was marked and annotated."

On the theme of his vanished library Aguilera was far from taciturn, and he recurred to this subject more than once in the days we spent together, but he volunteered no information about his relations in Madrid save in reply to a definite question.

"Yes, my mother's in Madrid. She's Scottish—born a Munro—and she regained her British nationality after my father died."

"Why doesn't she leave Madrid?"

"Oh, she's staying on to protect my sister and her children."

"Is your sister's husband still alive?"

"I don't know. He was on the General Staff. It's dangerous to try to get news. I expect he's been bumped off."

He said no more. Spaniards seldom speak of their relations behind the Red lines, for they would lose their sanity if they allowed their minds to dwell on these things.

Rain fell during our drive to Madrid, and we could see little more than the outline of the city from the Casa del Campo. Just behind the lines there is a house with an observation tower which commands, in fine weather, a magnificent panorama of Madrid. From this tower we could see (and be seen from) a tower, in possession of the Reds, about a mile and a half nearer Madrid.

"If it were fine," said Aguilera, "we should have to be careful. When the Reds see people moving about on this roof they assume that they are artillery officers and start shelling the house. There's the butt end of a 'seventy-five stuck in that wall. That's new since my last visit."

It was easy to understand why the Reds should shell our vantage post, less easy to understand why the house was still standing. In Flanders so ideal an observation tower within a mile of the front would not have survived for twenty-four hours, but in Flanders there was ammunition to squander, whereas in this war both sides have been severely rationed.

The next day we visited Toledo, just behind the front. Towns similarly situated in France and Flanders were uninhabitable, but the good folk of Toledo went about their business as in peace time. A spent bullet sometimes found its way into the open square in front of the Alcázar, but there was little else, save the crackle of desultory firing, to remind us that the Reds were on the other side of the Tagus.

It is only an occasional village such as Pozuelo, the scene of fierce fighting, where there has been destruction comparable to that on the Western Front. We visited Pozuelo, just after leaving Madrid, and one had to pick one's way with care.

"Don't touch that," said Aguilera, pointing to an unexploded grenade, "or you'll go to Hell. That is," he generously conceded, "unless you're in a state of grace."

But even the squalid litter of war had not wholly obliterated the personality of a charming country house. I picked a few violets from a flower-bed beside a gravel path where a rain-soaked book was lying. The morocco cover had detached itself, and the book, a study of Spanish literature in the Renaissance, had the sad appearance of an aristocrat in the gutter. The book lover does not think of a book as inanimate matter, and I was not surprised when Aguilera smoothed out its clammy pages with a caressing touch and carried it back into the shelter of the ruined house.

A rain-rotted basket-chair sagged into the unkempt lawn, and suddenly I realized what this garden must have looked like on a spring evening before the war. There would have been the scent of spring blossoms, instead of the faint odour of decaying matter, and the laughter of children at play, instead of the noisy bark of the machine-gun reverberating from just behind the garden wall. Perhaps, in the basket-chair, a scholarly old man would have puffed away at a cigar, absorbed in that study of Renaissance literature which Aguilera had just carried into the shelter.
καὶ σέ γέρον τὸ πρὶν μὲν ἄκούοεμεν ὀλβιον εἶναι.[1]

Just as we were leaving we stumbled on one of the minor casualties of this war; a little dog had fallen into a deep pit and was dying of starvation. He was making melancholy, panting noises, and he looked up at us with bewildered eyes.

[1] Achilles speaking to Priam: "And we hear that even you, old man, were once blessed."

"I wish I hadn't seen that," said Aguilera. "It will be dangerous to drag him out as lots of these dogs near the front have contracted rabies. I'll go and find a soldier, and have him shot."

The weather, meanwhile, had improved, and we decided to return towards Madrid. As we left Pozuelo I wondered what fate had befallen the kindly folk who lived in this quiet hamlet before the war.

I have just been reading an article in *Current History*, April, 1937, an American paper, fiercely anti-Franco. And this is what Mr. Ziffren has to say of life in Madrid:

> For some unknown reason, hats became taboo for both men and women. Someone said persons who wore hats were aristocrats, and therefore the enemies of the proletariat. . . . Fear of reprisals caused many Rightists, especially the young men, to shave off their moustaches, because the young Leftists regarded such hirsute decoration, also, as too aristocratic. Others went tieless and coatless in order to appear more proletarian, while still others sought to mask their identity with coloured glasses. . . . Foreigners were not molested by the militia unless they were suspected of hiding Spanish Rightists. . . . I believe it is fair to state that foreigners came off fairly well, generally speaking, although some Latin-Americans, possibly some Germans and Italians, got into serious trouble. A few, unfortunately, were killed. The murder of sisters of the Uruguayan Vice-Consul provoked the break of diplomatic relations between Spain and Uruguay.

"*Foreigners came off fairly well, generally speaking. . . .*" A lukewarm testimonial, riddled by damning qualifications. It is true that the sisters of the Uruguayan Vice-Consul were murdered, which was too bad, and as we have since learned, the Belgian *chargé d'affaires* was killed also; but *generally speaking*, if you were a foreigner you were *fairly safe*.

Of course, if you were *not* a foreigner . . . merely the

kind of Spaniard who did not normally go "tieless and coatless," your chances were less bright.

. . . . .

As we approached the observation tower, Aguilera said, "It's getting brighter, so they may shell us. I think I'll leave my car under the shelter of the house."

It was nice to feel that the house was some protection . . . to the car.

"We'd better be careful," said Aguilera, "they can spot us from that tower," and then added with charming inconsistency, "let's lunch up here."

We did.

A few seconds later the sun broke through the final defences of the mist, gleamed on the long façade of the Palace, and unshadowed the heart of Madrid. The reverberations of a trench-mortar dissipated the last rags of cloud still clinging to the University City, and revealed the wounded frontage of shell-shattered buildings.

Many years ago I fought my way down an Alpine peak through a driving snowstorm. During a momentary pause, as we lay exhausted on the rocks, the foreground of wind-driven snow suddenly sparkled into light. A puff of wind, the clouds parted, the sun came through, and eyes sick and tired of black rock and grey mist were gladdened by a sudden vista of green hills, blue lakes, and the bluer distances fading into the gold of sun-tinted clouds. Then the return of the sun meant the return of life and colour and warmth to a dark and stormy world, but the cruel sun of Madrid was like the arc lamp in an operating theatre, disclosing every detail of grim and savage wounds. Never, even among the mountains, have I felt, as I felt at Madrid, such a sense of personality behind inanimate things. The riven walls seemed like a wounded face through which a tortured soul found expression. The city radiated waves of human agony, the agony of those for whom every dawn was a hopeless dawn. I thought of men awaiting murder and women dreading rape, and the tragedy of desecrated churches. *Videte si est dolor sicut dolor meus.* I saw those words embroidered on a banner of Our Lady carried in the Easter procession at Seville, and thought of Madrid.

Captain Aguilera handed me his glasses.

"Look in line with that big tree. Just behind it you can see my house, or rather, what's left of it."

I took his glasses.

"Just ten minutes in a car from here," he said. "Just ten minutes. . . ."

And I knew that he was not thinking of the three thousand annotated books, or the manuscript that he had worked on for seven years.

Aguilera pointed out the tower of a famous church, and I was saddened by the thought of the "Real Absence" in churches where the Red Lamp has been extinguished by the Red fury. It was Palm Sunday, and I knew what Passion Week must mean to those for whom every street in Madrid is a veritable *Via Dolorosa.*

Martyrdom redeems the tragedy of Madrid. *Videte si est dolor. . . .* Yes, but there is beauty in the sorrow and nothing squalid. The Catholic pulse still beats in the arteries of Madrid. Red Spain has her Campions, for Red Spain is witnessing a revival of Elizabethan drama, the drama of the missionary priests. The newspaper, shared with such interest by two shabby down-at-heel proletarians, may be an improvised confessional, behind which a collarless priest gives absolution to a coatless penitent.

As I said farewell to that stricken city, I was ashamed that I could only pity where I should have envied those who are paying so grim a price for the authentic Christian experience, and I could only hope that persecution might conceivably discover in those of us who belong to the unheroic majority some strain of unsuspected fortitude.

The inescapable lesson of history is that Christianity was never intended to be a comfortable religion. There are periods when conformity is facile and fashionable, but the

Church seldom escapes for long the purge of persecution. Martyrdom is the test, and by that standard the Church in Spain has triumphed. It is not only the hierarchy and the priesthood that have died for their Faith. Many a slack and sinning Christian has discovered in these tragic months the inestimable value of a religion which meant little to him when it cost him little, and everything in the days when it has demanded everything.

9 TOLEDO AND THE ALCAZAR

On Monday Aguilera drove us to Toledo.

As we branched off from the Madrid road Aguilera remarked: "If we hadn't turned aside at this point to rescue the Alcázar garrison, we should have taken Madrid. At the time we didn't know that the Alcázar could have held out for another week."

"But if we'd taken Madrid," he added, "and left the Alcázar garrison to their fate, we'd have deserved to lose the war. But of course nothing could have stopped the army from taking the Toledo road. They'd have mutinied if they'd been told to march to Madrid."

As we drove towards Toledo, Foltz made a reference to the British prisoners at Talavera. Aguilera, who had seen them in their prison camp, said that they were inferior in fighting quality to the German and French volunteers. But the men he saw were not representative. Ralph Fox and John Cornford and the little group of fourteen, of whom Esmond Romilly and one other alone survive, fought with great gallantry. I am looking forward to reading Romilly's adventures in the International Brigade to be published this autumn.

I have read with great interest the moving description in *Single to Spain*[1] of the engagement in which practically every member of Romilly's group was killed. The author of this book resigned from the International Brigade because, as he frankly tells us, he could not stand the strain of war. His honesty in this personal record lends weight to his tribute to the heroism of the English who died in action.

The British Saklatvala battalion, seen by Aguilera both in action and in prison camp, seems to have been composed in the main of jobless unfortunates who had come to Spain because they had been offered well paid jobs behind the lines. They appear to have been only too grateful to the Nationalists for capturing them. In June General Franco released all the foreign prisoners he had captured and presented them with a small sum of pocket money for incidental expenses.

The Saklatvala battalion included only a small proportion of convinced Communists. Among them was a Red Cross youth from Birmingham. When he was captured he was actively engaged in binding up the wounds of some of the Nationalists. Foltz was impressed by this, but Aguilera was inclined to be cynical.

"After all," he said, "if he believed the usual Red lies that we shoot our prisoners, he would naturally have tried to make a good impression by concentrating on the Nationalist wounded."

As we approached Toledo I wondered whether the first view of the Alcázar would rank in memory with the great moments of travel, or be faintly disappointing. I shall not readily forget the first impact of Jerusalem, Rome, Venice or Athens, but these cities owe their appeal to the past, to great events which took place before we were born, whereas the Alcázar enshrines history experienced by us, if only at second hand.

---

[1] Keith Scott Watson: *Single to Spain.* New York, 1937.

I was in the American Middle West during the last phases of the siege, and owing to differences of time, I tuned in to the wireless every morning to hear the evening bulletins from Spain. We were all convinced that the garrison could not survive the explosion of the mines laid below the Alcázar.

I remember listening to a moving, though imaginary description of the last hour in the doomed Alcázar. Nothing I have heard over the wireless affected me more than this reconstruction, told with real feeling, of the last moments of the doomed garrison.

Arriving at Toledo, Aguilera went in search of a lady who had been in the siege, and we wandered off to the cathedral. The explosions had shattered the stained glass—otherwise the cathedral was undamaged. Aguilera's friend, Doña Carmen Aragones, lunched with us. She held an important position in a munition factory where girls were employed, and is a woman of thirty, the widow of an army officer who had died in Morocco five years before. Since his death she had lived in Toledo with her father, a personal friend of Colonel José Moscardó, the Commandant of the Alcázar. When the siege began she, her father, her children and her brothers joined the Alcázar garrison.

Doña Carmen enjoys life, and so does Aguilera, and the luncheon party was divided into two sections, a happy and hilarious minority spoke Spanish, and a disconsolate majority didn't. I did my best with a phrase book, a mixture of French, Latin and Italian, but it was a poor best. I am going to learn Spanish before I return to Toledo.

Doña Carmen is what all heroines should be, a beautiful heroine. She is infectiously vivacious, and only in rare moments when her face was in repose did one discover a hint of that iron tenacity which had sustained her through the siege. Aguilera told me that her gaiety and courage were contagious. "One loving soul," says St. Augustine, "sets another on fire," and courage is as contagious as love.

"I shall never forget," said Aguilera, "the first moment that I saw her. I penetrated into the Alcázar with the relieving force and tumbled into a dark vault, struck a match, and there she was with her children. She glanced up as the match flickered in the gloom, and I shan't forget the darkness of her eyes or the deathlike pallor of her face."

The "No surrender" spirit of the Alcázar permeated all aspects of the garrison life. The women were as ingenious in discovering substitutes for cosmetics as the men were in improvising defences against artillery fire. When all else failed Doña Carmen tried plaster from the walls as a substitute for face powder.

After lunch we went over the Alcázar, and visited the horrible underground vault where Doña Carmen and her children and the other women had slept in a cell only big enough for two; the swimming bath where the women had been transferred to be as far as possible from the place where the mines were expected to explode; the breeches in the wall through which the storming parties had attempted to force an entrance, and, most moving of all, the dark little office where Moscardó had talked on the telephone to his son just before he was shot by the Reds.

From a large window looking out across the Tagus we saw the houses now held by the Reds.

"There was an order a fortnight ago," said Doña Carmen, "forbidding anybody to stand at this window; we are within range of the Reds."

"Was the order recalled?" I asked Aguilera.

It seemed not. Nobody who had disobeyed the order had been killed, so the order had just lapsed. Spain is like that.

We explored the great crater exploded by the mine, and regretfully retraced our steps from the terrace into the town. As we did, I had a vision of a rebuilt Alcázar and a listless guide piloting a personally conducted party round its vaults, and repeating for the thousandth time a story which had thrilled him once, but had long since degenerated into a string of perfunctory words. The desultory firing beyond the Tagus was almost welcome as a reminder that war still protected the Alcázar from vulgar exploitation.

10 THE MIRACULOUS MARCH

M{AJOR} Geoffrey McNeill-Moss, in his book, *The Siege of the Alcázar*,[1] describes one of the greatest sieges in history with an impartiality that has been acclaimed even by reviewers of the Left.

This work has become a classic in military libraries, although one need not be a military man to enjoy the book. Some pages moved me more than anything I have read for many years. The emotion never degenerates into sentimentality; indeed something of the austerity of the Alcázar finds its way into his narrative.

The Republican siege of the Alcázar began on July 22, and was raised on September 27. On that date Colonel Moscardó, after having received an order from the Madrid Government to surrender the fortress, summoned his senior officers and certain of the leading civilians of Toledo to discuss the Government's demands. "Discuss" is not the correct word, for the rejection of this demand was inevitable. Seldom has a garrison started a siege with less hope of success. The revolt had failed in Barcelona and in Madrid. Franco was still separated from Spain by the

---

[1] Subsequently published as *The Epic of the Alcázar* (Knopf, 1939).

Straits of Gibraltar patrolled by the Red fleet. Within the garrison both food and water supplies would require the most rigid economy, and the means of defence at the disposal of the Alcázar was pitifully inadequate.

They had little hope of success, but the men prayed for and were granted a miracle. One can only follow in imagination the march of the relieving forces from the blue Straits of Gibraltar to the tawny cliffs that fall from the Alcázar to the Tagus.

The crossing of the Straits was a gamble only less glorious than the determination to land in Andalusia with a force so insignificant that nothing could have saved them had Andalusia been as red as the Reds believed.

Colonel Castejón set out on his career of conquest in a small ship with thirty-five selected officers. The Reds had counted with confidence on Andalusia, and it might well have seemed hopeless to land without an overwhelming force. There was no overwhelming force available. Colonel Castejón landed knowing that his venture of faith might end with a firing party, but his landing was unopposed, and the first chapter of the epic march closed without disaster. It is even possible that his heroic gesture turned the tide in Andalusia, for there is nothing that makes a greater appeal to the Spaniard than extravagances of courage.

Some weeks later Major McNeill-Moss met Colonel Castejón. His officers were particularly proud that since the force had landed in Spain they had never indented for a gun or a rifle or a round of ammunition. They were fighting their way through Spain with the rifles and ammunition brought with them from Morocco supplemented by what they had taken from the enemy in battle.

Meanwhile General Queipo de Llano had flown to Seville with a few officers. Outside the city he was joined by 183 supporters, soldiers and men of the Civil Guard. He commandeered lorries, drove to the Radio-Seville station and seized it.

"Faith in a fact," said William James, "often helps to

create a fact." De Llano, a fighting pragmatist, proves the truth of William James's dictum. He flooded the air with statements, fantastically untrue when made, but translated by his action into truth. Loud speakers in the cafés broadcasted his reckless statements into the streets. Colonel Castejón's audacious landing had created the atmosphere necessary to make the broadcast convincing. Rumour had multiplied the boatload of men who crossed the Straits into a phantom army of 40,000. De Llano summoned all Spaniards in Seville who loved Spain and hated anarchy to rally round him and to welcome the—wholly non-existent—army approaching the town. Meanwhile the Reds in the suburbs of Seville had brought artillery into action, and began to shell the town.

"Do you hear those guns?" shouted de Llano. "Listen to the glorious artillery of Spain routing the Red Marxist scum." The Red guns continued shooting, and the more noise they made the more panicky became their sympathizers listening in on the wireless. De Llano took Seville with the artillery of the Reds.

Seville was saved by the brilliance and courage of de Llano, and by the cowardice and incompetence of the Reds who outnumbered de Llano's hastily collected forces by at least a hundred to one. In England, unfortunately, General Queipo de Llano is less famous as the saviour of Seville than notorious as a broadcaster whose humour is condemned by our exacting standards of taste.

Few people in our country realize that his famous broadcasts are primarily intended to cheer and amuse the men at the Front. He speaks to them informally in a democratic style impossible in our own army. The soldiers love his Rabelaisian and bucolic wit, and their immense respect for the gallantry of the man who saved Seville by a miracle of courage and bluff is reinforced by their affection for a General who is incapable of pomposity. Old-fashioned Spaniards look down their noses at his more outrageous jests. He is fond of using a comic aside who interjects his own comments. "Caballero," begins the General, "is a . . . what did you say?" Murmurs off. "What's that? 'Caballero is a ——'." The Spanish word could be translated by less than five letters of our alphabet. Then after a pause the General adds in a tone of shocked dismay: "Oh, you know I couldn't *possibly* say that."

De Llano's broadcasts are addressed not only to Nationalists but to the Reds, who are forbidden to tune in to Seville, and who, because they are not only Red but Spanish, take a particular delight in ignoring this veto. De Llano's colourful character studies of the leading personalities of the Valencia Government are said to give even greater delight to the Reds than to the Nationalists.

The capture of Seville did nothing to solve the problem of transporting troops across a sea still commanded by the Red fleet. Some reinforcements were sent over by air, but this was a slow process, and on August 5 Franco decided that the time had come to repeat Castejón's exploit. Two mail steamers crowded with legionnaires and Moors, escorted by aircraft, an armed trawler and an obsolete gunboat, started across the Straits. A large government destroyer, armed with five 4-inch guns, challenged the convoy. The obsolete gunboat fired a few shots; a few bombs from the aeroplanes splashed into the sea, and Goliath retreated in panic. Castejón's handful of men had not waited for reinforcements. They had already covered many a breathless mile on their road to Toledo when Franco's troops began to cross the Straits.

Of all the myths propagated in this country by Reds and Pinks, none is more wholly fatuous than the legend of a hostile country cowed into submission by Franco's Moors. Every town and every village Castejón entered welcomed him as a deliverer. Had the peasants been hostile, his small force must inevitably have been surrounded and massacred, if not on disembarkation, at least within the early days of his advance. The Nationalists counted on popular support, and were not disappointed. They were forced to assume that their communications did not need to be protected, for there were no troops to protect them. Every normal military precaution was ignored because there was no alternative. The Alcázar had to be relieved. That was all that mattered. Through every town and every village the relieving force advanced at the incredible speed of more than twenty miles a day, overwhelming Government detachments that summoned up sufficient courage to remain and fight.

On August 11 they sighted Badajoz and on the 13th they took the town by storm.

The Badajoz garrison was about the same strength as the garrison that held Badajoz against Wellington. Wellington had 21,000 men at his disposal, Castejón little more than 3,000 men. Wellington had a siege train of fifty-two pieces at his disposal, Castejón four field guns. Yet Wellington, one of the greatest generals in British history, took eighteen days to capture Badajoz whereas Castejón stormed Badajoz after three days and captured it in thirteen hours of street fighting.

The name of Badajoz is associated in history with a massacre and this has stained the record of the victors. Here is the account of an eyewitness.

> Now commenced that wild and desperate wickedness which tarnished the lustre of the soldiers' heroism, for hundreds risked, and many lost, their lives trying to stop the violence. But the madness generally prevailed. And as the worst men are the leaders here, all the dreadful passions of human nature were displayed. Shameless rapacity, brutal intemperance, savage lust, cruelty, and murder, shrieks and piteous lamentations, groans, shouts, imprecations, the hissing of fires bursting from the houses, the crashing of doors and windows, and the reports of muskets used in violence, resounded for two days and nights in the streets of Badajoz. On the third, when

the city was sacked, when the soldiers were exhausted by their own excesses, the tumult rather subsided than was quelled. The wounded men were then looked to and the dead disposed of.

I am quoting, not as the reader might imagine, from the files of the *New Statesman* but from Napier's *History of the Peninsular War*, for the only massacre ever to take place in Badajoz was a massacre of the Spanish garrison by British troops. The mythical massacre attributed to the Nationalists in this war was described by an "eyewitness" who was in Portugal at the time.

Any troops but Spanish would have demanded a rest after the thirteen hours of stubborn street fighting, the last phase in the fight for Badajoz, but there was no rest for the men who were to save the Alcázar. On the morning of the 16th they were off again. On August 9 they had reached Oronza, having advanced 250 miles in three weeks, captured Badajoz and fought more than twenty minor actions on the way.

Suvorov's Alpine march has often been described as the greatest military march in history, but Suvorov has been eclipsed by Castejón.

I borrow, with Major McNeill-Moss's permission, a vivid description of Castejón's column on the march from his book, *The Siege of the Alcázar*, published by Knopf.

> Ahead comes as scout, an improvised armoured car, captured from the enemy: a space: three or four touring cars with legionaries and machine-guns: another space: then the main body, a main body carried in the strangest fleet of motor coaches that it is possible to imagine. They have been impressed where found and are gaily coloured, in peasant and small-town taste; scarlet, white, bright blue, orange, apple green, purple, pink. They are packed with armed men. Forty coaches of legionaries: forty coaches of Moors: eight lorries of ammunition, perhaps with two field-guns in them: another

forty coaches of legionaries: a wireless signal waggon, hastily contrived; an ambulance or two: a tank-waggon for motor spirit: a touring car with machine-guns trained to the rear.

Upon the roofs of all the coaches is the baggage; mattresses of every colour—for the Spaniard who will fight starving and unpaid, hates to lie hard; bundles in counterpanes, in women's shawls, in gay striped blankets; valises, items of loot—for of all the world's looters the Moor is king; a coop of hens; a parrot in a cage; a nanny-goat in milk; a net of melons; then, perhaps on every twentieth roof-top, three men lounging beside an anti-aircraft gun, cocked skyward, ready to fire.

Fastened to the radiators are religious mascots; a crucifix found in a wrecked church; a Blessed Virgin with crown of cracker jewels—and perhaps beside her, placed there without a thought of irreverence or incongruity, a Mickey Mouse.

The legionaries are in khaki shirts, short-sleeved, with gilt-embroidered badges on black tabs, with bandoliers, slung rifles, tasseled glengarry caps of khaki drill. They have taut faces, burnt with the sun, plastered with white dust. They are fit, alert, confident, conscious of being masters of their trade, certain of victory; and, knowing that, cheerful and gay.

The Moors are solemn and patient. Sometimes at this or that unusual sight they may be momentarily curious. They are as a rule not much darker than the Spaniards, but there is a certain grey or yellow tinge under the dry walnut pigment of their skin. They are shanky, hollow-cheeked, sinewy. They are polite. They seldom smile. They walk softly, and with the forward thrust of animals that live dangerously. They wear the baggy trousers of their corps, turbans, and open tunic-shirts.

In battle the legionaries advance in those short baggling rushes which only the finest infantry, once down, will rise to, when under fire. The Moors in battle work upon their stomachs and wriggle forward at a reptilian speed. Upon the line of route, they sit huddled in their blanket-like burnouses; for, when not active, they seem always cold.

. . . . .

The tactics of such a column had been devised to suit the conditions of this campaign. The enemy had always the advantage of numbers; but no knowledge, little skill, no final steadiness. For the Nationalists the game was bluff; audacity; manœuvre; speed. And the battle was always the same.

The leading armoured car breasts a rise. The road stretches on, grey asphalt powdered with dust, and on each side emptiness. A mile ahead there is a village; one-storeyed, mud-walled, clustering around a lofty dusty Baroque church. The armoured car slows and sends back a signal. There are two flashes from the village, bright even in the sunlight. Guns! The village held!

Two shells sing. They burst high overhead. The armoured car stops. Its driver finds reverse. The car drones slowly back behind the skyline. The plain is empty once again; stubble, dry maize, scorched prairie, rolling land the colour of a horse's mane, stupendous distances, a range of hills, coral pink and far away; horizon; blue sky; silence.

Behind the slope the coaches close up and stop. The legionaries are out. The Moors are out. The plan is ready; 'Sealed Pattern Order of Attack'—to meet—'Sealed Pattern Village with Sealed Pattern Order of Defence.' A little party with machine-guns doubles out, clears the road, and makes ready to advance, astride it. A battalion with its machine-guns is doubling out into the empty land that stretches for ever to the left. Another battalion is doubling out upon the other side into the emptiness that stretches to the right.

The battalion in reserve—'less the party with machine-guns on the road'—takes position, scattered in little groups. The wireless in a lorry has reported and is calling for planes.

Now the empty coaches are all in reverse, creeping back cautiously, clear of the fight. The anti-aircraft guns are ready, waiting. The commander of the force draws near behind the hill-crest, and with him goes a little group of men with field-glasses.

The word is given. The centre party with its machine-guns breaks cover over the ridge and, well extended, goes forward on each side of the road; cautious but never checking. For some time they continue on their way. The field-guns on the village fringe bark at them. Then all at once the mud walls of the village blaze with rifle and machine-gun fire; and from the trenches, scraped in the fields on left and right, and up till now unseen, a furious fusillade begins. The men of the centre party throw themselves down. Their machine-guns come into action.

For half an hour the air whistles with bullets. Once or twice the commander of the columns crawls to the crest line of the ridge, to see that everything is progressing according to plan. To left and right the flanking battalions have trotted out. Now they are a mile, or more, outside the farthest trenches of the enemy. They face 'front' again, and order their advance, so as to pass a mile wide on each side of the village. The town-bred volunteers catch sight of them and, after shouting and pointing, bring their rifles round. The range is fifteen hundred yards. At this distance such rifle-men are hardly dangerous. The bullets sing over-head. Now and then one falls short, flicks up the dust and goes by, humming.

The advance goes on round either flank. Now the machine-guns in the village cannot fire at the advancing troops, who are already too far round for them. The volunteers within the village look about them, wondering what will happen next. Planes have been called for by their commander, also. But in an army of eager amateurs messages arrive, or not, according to their luck. The artillerymen on the village fringe grow restless. They clank the drop-fronts of their ammunition limbers shut. Presently they begin man-handling the guns out of position. The rifle-men hear that sound. So the guns are off? Some fire faster. Some look about them. A few slink back.

Now the flanking battalions of the Nationalists can see clear behind the village. They halt, lie down, make ready their machine-guns.

In the village all is confusion. The Marxists have gone into committee. Syndicalists are keeping up their fire. Anarchists favour a forward movement and a charge, at any cost. But soon the less courageous of the militia-men are slinking back. Someone tries to stop them. An argument ensues, bitter, wordy. Others come up and take part in it. Someone in comparative authority forms a party and starts it off towards the rear. But at such times a formed body moving rearward is like a magnet. Stragglers dribble out after it. Presently the exit of the village is like the exit of a cinema, after the show. The militia-men trot away. Some motors in the village are sounding horns, perhaps to rally the troops, perhaps to get the road clear for themselves. Presently the retreat is general; and in no order at all. Three, four, five thousand men; all keeping to the asphalt road which runs ahead of them, over the naked countryside.

Out on the flanks are the Nationalist machine-gunners. They have been waiting long for this. They open fire. Their bullets intersect upon the road, at a spot perhaps half a mile behind the village. The volunteers' retreat becomes a rout, and all press on, but no man can pass the zone beaten by the machine-guns' fire. Those near the front of the retreating crowd halt and recoil from the corpses of their comrades, lying in the road; those behind press forward, clamouring. There comes a moment when the surging mass bursts forward like a flood. It forms the perfect target. Two of the guns keep up their cross-fire. The others traverse. The militia-men go down like dry thistles before a scythe. At last they realize the road is death. They scatter from it, out into the fields where they are lost indeed.

Four planes come droning up from the south. They part and swing wide from the village, two on each side of it. Flying low, they drop some little bombs, well on the flanks of the scattered militia-men. They circle round, closing in, dropping their bombs, shepherding these townsmen back to the road again.The leaders of the rout take to the asphalt. The going is easier. They have dropped their rifles; they struggle out of bandoliers and toss them aside. They are out of breath. They jostle each other as they run. They keep to the road. When they are thick enough, the planes wheel round and swoop low, machine-gunning them. The pursuit goes on till there seems nothing left worth chasing. For two, three, perhaps four miles the road is dotted with dead and dying.

. . . . .

Behind the village the centre detachment of the Nationalists has closed, and packed its machine-guns. The flanking battalions are legging it, back across the open land to where their transport waits for them. Sometimes, passing a saint or Blessed Virgin on a radiator, they will touch the medallions dangling outside their shirts, or cross themselves. They climb back into the coaches and settle down. Ready!

Not quite. Sometimes the Government commander, farther

back, will rush up another motorized column to retrieve the day. The men will clamber out and come forward again with a ragged valour. The legionaries will extend a little wearily, lie flat, and mow them down with fire. There will be delay, and another half-dozen casualties among the Nationalists. A coach will somehow be set on fire, and in the end, when the counter-attack is broken, there will be another five hundred militia-men who will not fight again.

The column forms. The coaches are ready; many-coloured, stretched incongruously like a variegated paper streamer across this tawny field of war.

The armoured cars move on, stopping sometimes to clear the road of dead and dying militia-men. They pull bodies to the side and leave them. There they will lie for weeks, horrible, worried by dogs at night, stinking in the sunlight. The column moves on and leaves them. Toledo and the Alcázar are still a hundred miles away, and the little Army of Africa has neither men enough nor time to bury the dead.

11 THE EPIC OF THE ALCÁZAR

Θάνατον εἰσορῶ πέλας Ἱερέα Θανόντων[1]
Euripides.

WHAT MANNER OF MEN were these who held the Alcázar while columns of relief forced their way northward from the Gibraltar Straits?

Colonel José Moscardó, the Commandant, was a middle-aged soldier who had lived in semi-retirement for some time. When the War broke out he was military Governor of the province. "He was a tall, reserved, gentle-mannered man," writes Major McNeill-Moss. "He had a strict sense of duty. He was religious. In a nation where most were slack, he was exact."

Roman astringency has made the Latin language a most economical medium for the expression of thought, and it has left its mark on the Iberian peninsula. Let me cite a characteristic Spanish story from Salamanca.

Fray Luis de León had been acquitted after four years' imprisonment by the Inquisition. He was escorted in triumph to his lecture room where a vast audience awaited him expectantly, hoping for a moving account of his sufferings. The friar got up, glanced round the crowded hall and began his lecture.

---

[1] I see Death the High Priestess of the Dead standing by.

"As we were saying yesterday . . ."

He then took up the argument of his lecture where it had been cut short four years before.

The men of the Alcázar were economical in verbal heroics but extravagant in heroic deeds. A few brief words attributed to Colonel Moscardó will be quoted so long as Spain endures.

When the telephone rang in the small dark office, lined with photographs of men who had commanded the Alcázar in less stirring times, Moscardó picked up the receiver and a voice at the other end informed him that his son had been captured by the Reds and would be shot unless Moscardó surrendered the Alcázar. When the boy came to the telephone and asked his father what to do, Moscardó is reported to have said, "Commend thy soul to God, my son, cry 'Viva España!' and die like a patriot. The Alcázar does not surrender!"

The boy was shot, but not before he had expressed his great affection and love for his father, and his willingness to do as he was commanded. Moscardó lost a son but saved his garrison. He is said to have greeted the colonel who relieved the Alcázar with the words, "No change to report."

No change. The garrison had not changed hands. The old flag of Christian Spain, red and yellow, continued to fly over the shattered shell of the Alcázar.

During the siege the outside world believed that the Alcázar was garrisoned exclusively by young cadets. This was not so, for the siege started while the cadets were on leave and only seven of them endured the siege. The tributes paid by the world to the heroic cadets were more than earned by young soldiers who fought with memorable courage.

The Civil Guard formed the largest group in the garrison. Six hundred of them served under their own officers and their own commander, whose brilliance and fertility of invention played an important part in the siege. The garrison included 150 army officers whose average age was between seventeen and eighteen, rather less than the average of the cadets. There were 35 Phalangists, 10 Carlists, 25 members of the Monarchist Association, and 40 peasants and workmen, a total of 1,028 for the garrison. This number included 670 non-combatants:—100 men too old to serve, 520 women, and 50 children.

The garrison was well supplied with rifles and with small-arms ammunition. They had twelve machine-guns, none less than fourteen years old. They possessed two light guns with a dozen rounds of ammunition, and one small trench mortar, with severely-limited ammunition. The guns and the trench mortar were too precious to be used excepting at a crisis. There was also a very limited stock of bombs.

For all practical purposes the Alcázar was defended by machine-guns and rifles against big guns, aeroplanes, trench-mortars, flame-throwers and tanks.

The garrison were on very short rations throughout the siege. One horse or one mule was killed daily to provide soup for the entire garrison. The daily ration of gritty hard bread was so small that it could be "completely covered by a cupped hand." The drinking water was doled out at the rate of a litre a day. There was no water for washing. Doña Carmen mentioned this as one of the major hardships of the siege. Among the minor hardships was the lack of light. Mule or horse fat provided a substitute for candles, but as only one mule or one horse was killed daily, the supply of fat was limited, and lighting was confined to places where light was essential. The women and children spent most of their time in darkness.

On September 9 Major Vincente Rojo approached with a white flag. He was blindfolded and taken into the Alcázar. He had been both a cadet and an officer instructor in the Academy, and he cannot have felt very happy as he was led to the Commandant. His mission was to offer the garrison their lives if they would surrender. His proposal was rejected, but when he left he asked Moscardó if he could convey any requests to those outside. The end seemed near and the mines under the Alcázar were nearly ready.

Moscardó asked that a priest might be sent to the garrison to baptize children born during the siege. The Government agreed to this request, and the priest selected for this mission was Canon Vásquez Camarasa.

A Spanish Bishop who had heard Canon Camarasa preach tells me that he was one of the most rhetorical preachers in Spain. He was most popular, and could and did demand very high fees for a sermon.

Before the Revolution he was known to sympathize with the Left Wing, and to this he owed his life. He was the only priest who was allowed to leave Red Spain after the outbreak of war. When he arrived in Paris he published a letter denouncing the Communists, and defending his own record. The Canon's *apologia* convinced me but made no impression at all in Nationalist Spain. Of the priests in Toledo, only seven who were in hiding escaped massacre. The Nationalists can scarcely be blamed for suspecting the sincerity of any priest, other than a Basque, who is on friendly terms with the Reds.

The Canon was criticized, among other things, for leaving the garrison with no further hope of the Sacrament at a time when they were expecting sudden death. To this he answered that he had promised to return, that he could not break his word, that if he did break his word the Government would take prompt revenge on priests in their power.

There is no reason to suspect the sincerity of priests with Left-Wing sympathies before the outbreak of the war, and when the war broke out it was natural that Canon Camarasa, who had professed belief in the Popular Front, should avoid attacking it. It was certainly tempting to postpone his ultimate denunciation of the Government's crimes until he had bought his right to leave Red Spain by appearing to condone those crimes. He chose the path of compromise, and only those who are confident that they would have preferred martyrdom may fairly blame him.

Canon Camarasa visited the Alcázar in lay dress so as not to provoke his allies. He baptized the newly born babies and celebrated Mass, and all those present, having fasted and confessed, received Holy Communion. The Canon then, with that eloquence which had made him so famous a preacher, warned all present of inevitable doom if they refused to surrender. Here again he may have spoken as he did because he was a kindly well-meaning man who wished to save those who could still be saved, or, as his critics maintain, because he had been charged by the Reds to secure, at all costs, the surrender of the Alcázar.

All those who heard him believed that they had received the final Sacrament and that death was imminent.

That evening Major Rojo returned and offered the evacuation of the women and children. Four representatives of the women were sent for and asked to consult the other women and to bring back their answer.

Let us follow these women down into the vaults of the Alcázar, where they were to debate the offer of life. None of them expected to survive if they stayed, for both within and without the Alcázar it was expected that the mines would destroy the garrison.

It is not easy to wait for a lingering death. Every night these women could hear the insistent burr of pneumatic drills where the mines were being laid below the vaults. When the burr ceased they woke from fitful slumber as if warned that the sudden silence was the prelude to an explosion.

Time has a disintegrating effect on courage. Only women of heroic stamina could endure for seven days what these women endured for seven weeks: seven weeks on horrible food and insufficient water; seven weeks cooped up in dark, dank cells; seven weeks of sleeplessness. Doña Carmen told me that among the major trials of the siege was the noise. Three feet of stone ceiling separated the vault where she slept from a courtyard regularly shelled. The clatter of the falling columns mingled with the explosions, each one of which seemed to be bursting exactly behind her head.

The women in the Alcázar refused to entertain the suggestion that they would leave. Major Rojo's representatives returned with the unanimous reply that the women of the Alcázar would not desert their men, and even if their own men wished to surrender, they would oppose this action. If necessary they would follow the example of the women of Saragossa who in the siege of 1808 took up arms and manned the defence.

Within the Alcázar the women and children had been moved to the swimming baths furthermost from the mining operations.

At 6:20 a.m. on September 18 the rifle fire ceased, and there was a great silence. In the Log Book of the Alcázar a line was drawn underneath the last entry and underneath was written, "All possible having been done, we commend ourselves to God."

On the ridges north of the town pressmen had their notebooks on their knees, cinematograph men were poised and alert. These kindly folk waited not only with excitement but with sympathy, for they believed that all those in the garrison would die.

A stir of expectancy passed through the spectators. The Minister of War pressed a button and the roar of the explosion shattered the silence of the hills. The last fragments of the southwest tower, a hundred feet high, cascaded in tumbling boulders down the slope, and there were some who sighed to think of young men butchered to make a Moscow holiday.

They sighed too soon. The casualties of the garrison were

slight. Only eighteen were killed in the fighting that followed, and only two in the actual explosion. Before long the escarpments of the Alcázar were red with the blood of men mown down by the furious fire of the unconquerable defenders. Within twelve minutes of the explosion three enormous breaches had been blown in the defences of the Alcázar. Men weakened by privation climbed desperately on the the disintegrating masonry of shattered walls. The breaches were held, and one more miracle was added to the miracles already inscribed in the record of the Alcázar.

On September 27 the garrison was relieved. They had food for a few more days. They had five mules and one horse.

More than once in telling the story of the Alcázar I have used the word "miracle," and I have used it because no other word has seemed adequate. Nobody can follow the story of the column of relief, from its first passage across the Straits dominated by the Red fleet to the walls of Toledo, without realising that at every stage of the amazing march the odds against success were overwhelming.

Toledo lies in a loop of the Tagus, and a line of trenches dug along this loop must have delayed the relieving force for weeks. Meanwhile the Alcázar would have been forced to surrender owing to lack of food. This elementary precaution was neglected. No trenches were dug, and the overwhelming majority of the Red army fled in confusion.

Not once but many times the garrison had survived an attack which, if resolutely pressed home, must inevitably have succeeded. Again and again the column of relief gambled, and every gamble came off. They were lucky. That is one way of putting it. But there is another explanation to reconcile with the mathematical theory of chance: "This is the Lord's doing, and it is marvellous in our eyes."

There were moments when the Alcázar garrison dared to hope that they might be relieved, but these moments were short-lived. They were content to fight on, not only because they were helping Spain by immobilising a large force of Reds, but because there are some defeats more glorious than victory. The Alcázar might fall but it would never surrender, and the captured shell would remain as a symbol of the Saving Spirit of Christian Spain.

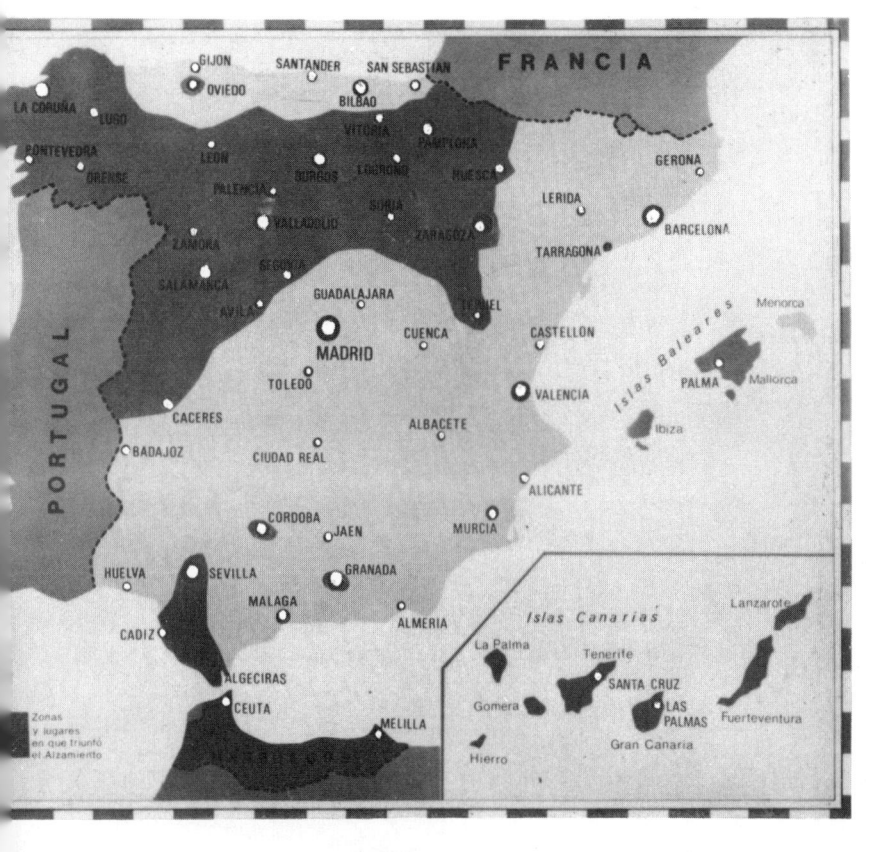

Division of Spain at the start of the Civil War, July, 1936. Darker areas show territory held by Franco; lighter areas are Republican.

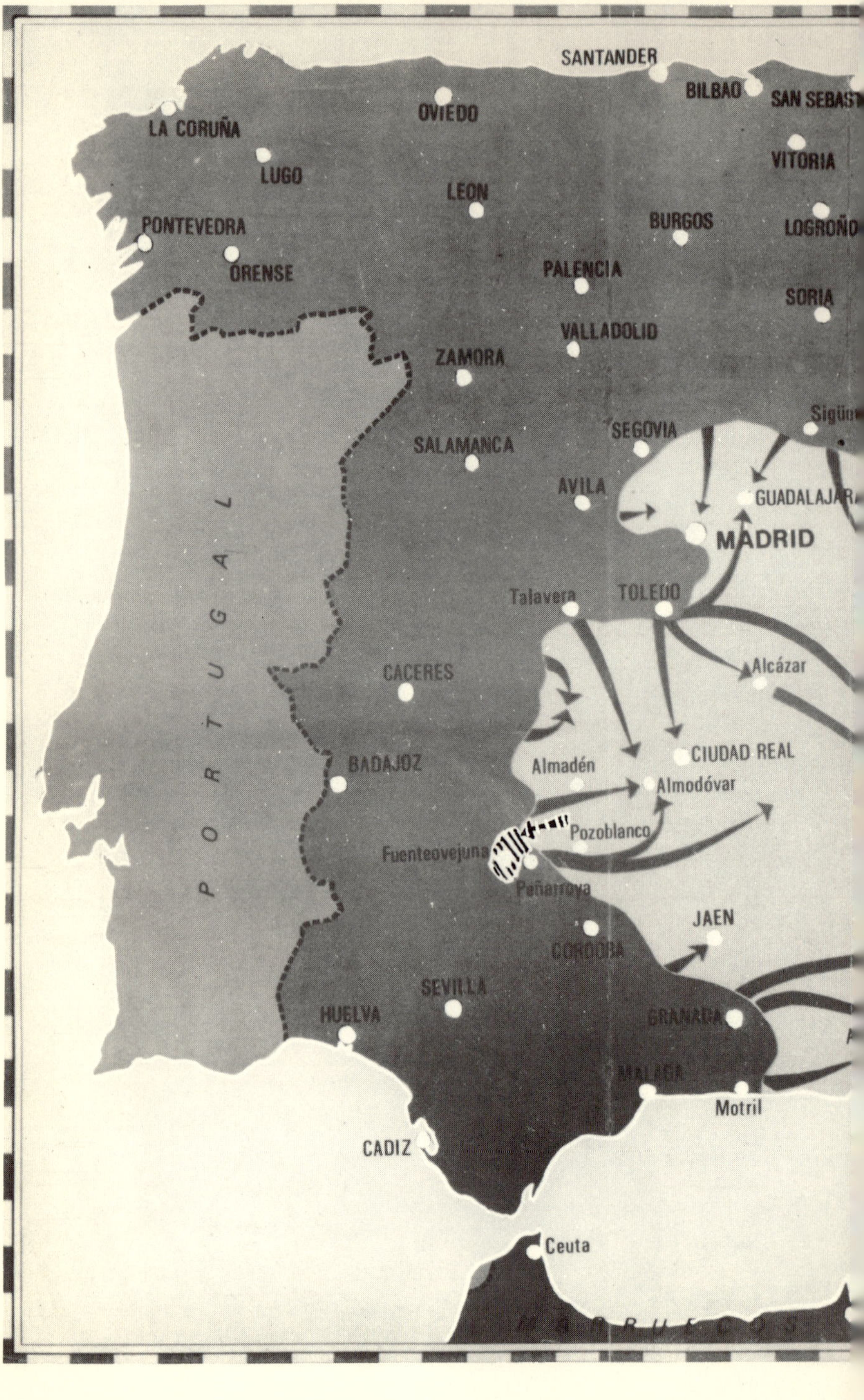

SANTANDER
BILBAO
SAN SEBAST
LA CORUÑA
OVIEDO
LUGO
VITORIA
LEON
PONTEVEDRA
BURGOS
LOGROÑO
ORENSE
PALENCIA
SORIA
VALLADOLID
ZAMORA
SEGOVIA
SALAMANCA
AVILA
GUADALAJARA
MADRID
PORTUGAL
Talavera
TOLEDO
Alcázar
CACERES
CIUDAD REAL
Almadén
BADAJOZ
Almodóvar
Pozoblanco
Fuenteovejuna
Peñarroya
JAEN
CORDOBA
SEVILLA
HUELVA
GRANADA
MALAGA
Motril
CADIZ
Ceuta
MARRUECOS

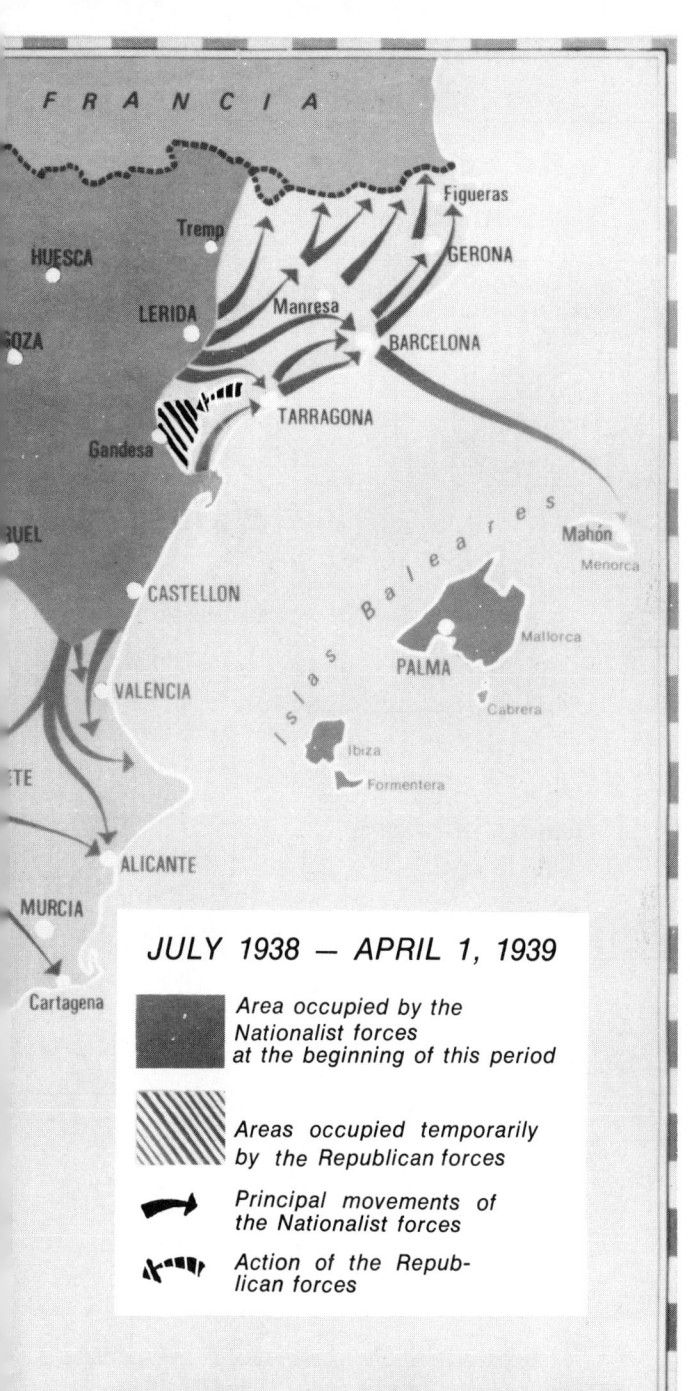

The final action, from July, 1938 to war's end, April 1, 1939.

JULY 1938 — APRIL 1, 1939

Area occupied by the Nationalist forces at the beginning of this period

Areas occupied temporarily by the Republican forces

Principal movements of the Nationalist forces

Action of the Republican forces

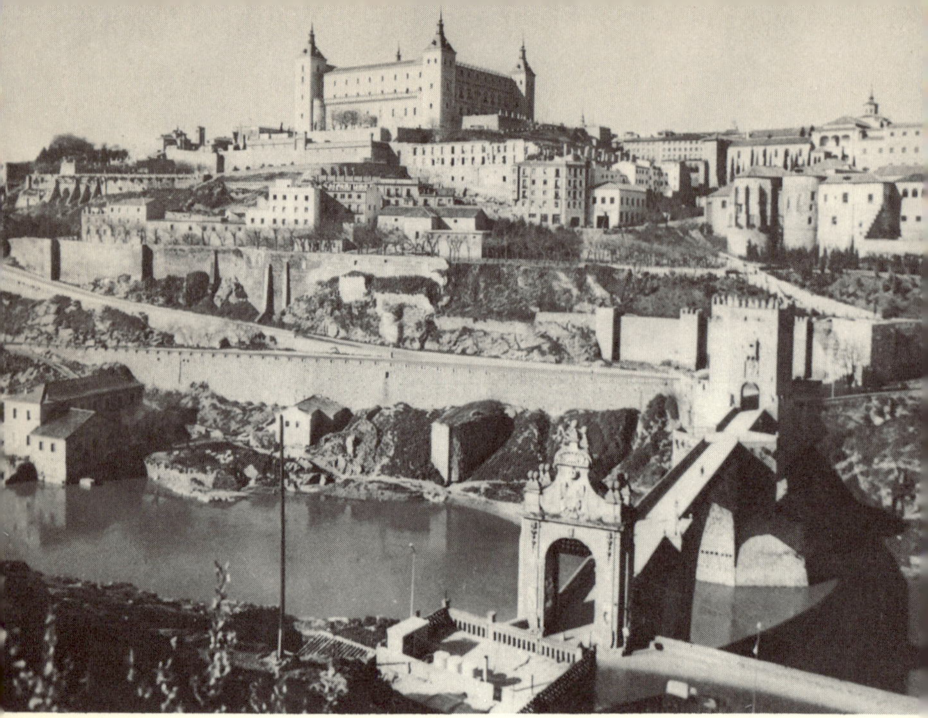

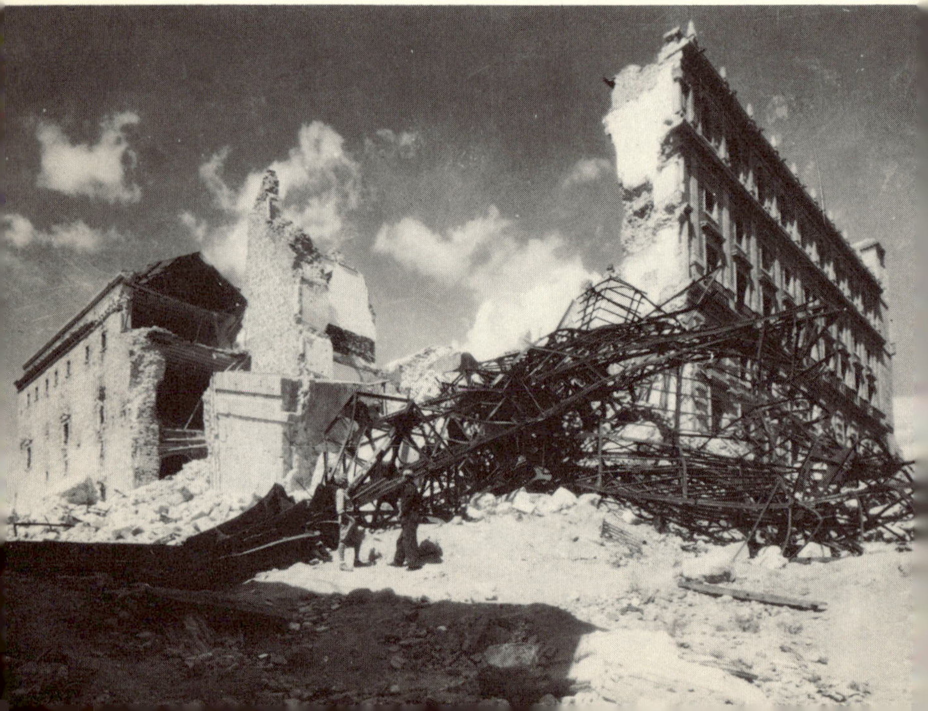

Communists saluting the Republican flag of the 10th International Brigade. The colors are red, yellow and purple. The crowns of the traditional flag have been replaced by castles. This was the flag used between 1931 and 1939 by the Republicans.

(*Opposite top.*) The Alcázar (Toledo) before the siege. Spain's military academy, the equivalent of ours at West Point, was originally a Moorish structure, later becoming the residence of Emperor Charles V. The Nationalists took refuge there in July of 1936 when the Republicans laid siege to it.

(*Left.*) The Alcázar was relieved in September of 1936. Much of it had been destroyed. (Alcázar means "the castle" in arabic.)

The Carmelite Church in Barcelona, sacked by the Reds, showing ancient mummies of Nuns vandalized.

Colonel (later General) José Moscardó, who commanded the Alcázar. It was he who, when the Republicans threatened to shoot his 19-year old son unless he yielded, is reported to have said: "Commend thy soul to God, my son, cry '¡Viva España!' and die like a patriot. The Alcázar does not surrender." The son was shot.

Generalísimo Francisco Franco. The picture was taken in about 1

12 FROM TALAVERA TO SEVILLE

I SAID GOOD-BYE to Aguilera with keen regret. His general philosophy had enlightened, and his scholarship instructed, me during our days spent together. I hope we shall meet again.

Señor Herrero of the Press Bureau at Talavera very kindly offered to drive me to Merida. My friend was a keen Carlist, and he sniffed indignantly at the suggestion that the old régime had been backward and slow to reform. On the contrary, he assured me, Primo de Rivera had instituted far more radical reforms during his brief period of power than any of the Liberal Governments in the last hundred years.

Our driver was something of a freak. He not only sounded his horn before reaching the corner, but even cornered on the right side of the road. At only one point during our journey did he remind me of Aguilera. He suddenly stepped on the accelerator and the car bounded forward, a justifiable acceleration for at this point we were only separated by little more than a mile or so from the Red lines.

The front in Spain is very thinly held. For mile after mile there are no trenches, and the line is secured by outposts separated by varying intervals. In these circumstances infiltration is tempting, and raiders not infrequently steal through the outposts, loot a few chickens, fire a few shots and then return to their own lines. An Irish newswoman had a narrow escape from the Reds while motoring near the front. Her car was riddled with bullets, and she was lucky to escape with her life. Sometimes an airman swoops down, destroys a car with his machine-gun, and disappears.

At one point we had a choice of route, the shorter near the Red lines. We asked an elderly Carlist in a village for his advice. He motioned us on. The short cut was safe, he insisted. We had nothing to fear. This meant only that the Reds had not raided that particular section of the road for some time, no more and no less reassuring than that none of those who had defied the official regulations and continued to look out of the Alcázar windows towards the Tagus, had as yet been shot.

From Merida, I travelled by train to Seville and arrived in the early hours of the morning. I was lucky to get a bed in a small hotel near the station, and next day I transferred to the Andalusia. I stayed in Seville through Easter week.

13 BATTLE AGAINST CHAOS

A PASSAGE in *Greeks and Barbarians* has a certain relevance to the war in Spain. The author, Professor J. A. K. Thomson, is an inspiring critic of Hellenism and a brilliant translator. Few renderings combine, as his does, accuracy with felicity of expression.

> Heroes of ancient story are alike in their championship of law and order. I suppose the two most popular and representative were Heracles and Theseus. Each goes up and down Greece and Barbary destroying *hybristai*, local robber-kings, strong savages, devouring monsters, ill customs and every manner of 'lawlessness' and 'injustice.' In their place each introduces Greek manners and government, Law and Justice. It was this which so attracted Greek sympathy to them and so excited the Greek imagination. . . . As for us, our sympathies are ready to flow out to the picturesque defeated monsters—the free Centaurs galloping on Pelion—the cannibal Minotaur lurking in his Labyrinth. But then our bridals are not liable to be disturbed by raids of wild horsemen from the mountains, nor are our children carried off to be dealt with at the pleasure of a foreign monarch. People who meet with such experiences get surprisingly tired of them. There is a figure known to mythologists as a Culture Hero. He it is who is

believed to have introduced law and order and useful arts into the rude community in which he arose. Such heroes were specially regarded, and the reverence felt for them measures the need of them. Thus in ancient Greece we read of Prometheus and Palamêdes, the Finns had their Wainomoinen, the Indians of North America their Hiawatha. Think again of historical figures like Charlemagne and Alfred, like Solon and Numa Pompilius, even Alexander the Great. A peculiar romance clings about their names. Why? Only because to people fighting what must often have seemed a losing battle against chaos and night, the institution and defence of law and order seemed the most romantic thing a man could do. And so it was.

To the Englishman there is nothing romantic about a policeman. They accept him as if he were a natural phenomenon like the sunrise. They take law and order for granted. Our island has been invaded since the Conquest and its revolutions have been but few in number and mild in character.

The secure and comfortable atmosphere of our island dulls the critical faculty, and very few Englishmen have lived through a reign of Red terror such as the terror in Russia, in Bavaria during the period of Communist control in 1919, in Hungary under Bela Kun, or in Spain during the four months of anarchy following the return to power of the Popular Front. Though we have given Europe its greatest imaginative literature, we are not, as a whole, an imaginative people. We find it difficult to translate continental terrorism into English terms, but the effort is worth making.

After the February elections of 1936, Arthur Bryant, one of the great modern English historians, writes in *The Observer*:

> When a so-called 'Popular Front' Government, with an electoral minority in the country but a majority in the Cortes, was formed only to capitulate to its own extreme elements, the

work of Communist agitators went on unchecked. Lists were prepared of those who were to be killed in every place, preparatory to the revolutionary assumption of power on the usual Marxist lines. In hundreds of towns and villages off the beaten track, the most degraded members of the local community, spurred on by the agents of the International, instituted a reign of terror. Murders, robberies, rapes, and burnings, provided they were exercised in the sacred name of the clenched fist and the proletarian dictatorship, passed unpunished and unrebuked by the Government. In Málaga alone, according to the testimony of a British resident, every church in the place (some forty in all, with the exception of the cathedral and two small buildings) had been burnt before the outbreak of the civil war. And this in a country where popular Catholic feeling, to put it on its lowest basis, is certainly as strong as it is in Britain. Should we call the law-abiding, religious elements in Hull or Huddersfield Fascists if they took up arms against a Government which had allowed and openly encouraged a mob of hooligans to burn down every Noncomformist chapel in the town, and threaten death to all who would not shout their slogan? Can a Liberal like Franco, who supported the republican revolution of 1931, be justly accounted a Fascist and a reactionary because he took his life in his hands and headed a popular rising of the more responsible elements in the community against a Government that permitted such a state of anarchy? What Englishman, given the same conditions, would not have done the same?

These things seem very remote from English life, but it is by no means certain that we shall continue to escape from the periodic waves of Red terror which sweep from time to time over Europe, and we may be sure that even the mildest form of Red Terrorism in England or America would transform most of the amiable "pinks" who to-day are abusing Franco into ardent supporters of law and order. They will probably be among the first to scream for an "Anglo-Saxon Franco" to save them.

To the arm-chair observer revolutions may seem rather

romantic, but "people who endure such experiences get extraordinarily tired of them," so tired that they are ready to follow the first leader who will offer them what Heracles and Theseus offered the Greeks. This is the cause of that devotion to Mussolini and Hitler so puzzling to people who have never known insecurity.

I have often asked supporters of democracy why they should object to a democratic country freely electing a dictator and entrusting that dictator with powers. I sometimes suspect that our Progressives regard a foreign country as "democratic" if it is ready to accept a form of Government approved by English radicals, and undemocratic if it is perverse enough to prefer the kind of Government desired by the majority of its citizens.

I do not believe that dictatorships can ever be more than a temporary expedient in any great European country. Fascism has never arisen in Europe as a spontaneous movement, but only as a reaction against Red terror. *England and the United States will only turn to Fascism if those who to-day are loudest in their denunciation of Fascism ever succeed in destroying our confidence in democracy.* If Anti-Fascists spent less time attacking Mussolini and more energy counteracting Communism, the future of Anglo-Saxon democracy would be less uncertain.

There is a kind of Liberal intellectual who travels with deputations to other countries, and professes himself an enthusiastic admirer of internationalism, but who never mentally leaves England. He cannot escape from that climate of security in which he has always lived. He never really meets foreigners; foreigners meet him, on his plane and at his level. He never sees foreigners as human beings but as abstractions passionately interested in concepts such as democracy, universal suffrage, or Socialism. He cannot escape from his own shadow, the shadow cast by the sun of Victorian prosperity. He forgets that even in England politically minded people are the exception. Many Englishmen never vote at all, and many of those who do vote, vote in a perfunctory fashion. They suspect that the essential nature of the Government they live under will not be radically changed whether they send a National Conservative or a supporter of the Labour Party to Westminster. Life, so they think, will go on much as it did before whatever happens. Crime, sex and sport, will, as before, provide the papers with news about things that matter. Property will be respected and burglars and murderers will be hunted and captured and convicted and condemned to death or imprisonment, and the police will do their duty. The accepted framework of a civilised society will be maintained.

Let us clear our minds of cant. Democracy has been comparatively successful in Great Britain, because, and only because, Conservatives, Labour and Liberals have been prepared to govern *within the framework of common principles.* The difference between the parties is a difference of emphasis and not a difference of principle. Democracy of the English kind cannot and will not work in Spain, for the Spaniard does not understand compromise. No country can prosper under a régime of alternating socialism and conservatism. Democracy works in England, but in Spain democracy degenerates into Red Revolution. Democracy is possible in England because the English play cricket, and they carry into practice the philosophy of cricket. The great-hearted British public decide that one particular team has been batting long enough, and that it's time that the other crowd had their innings too. Politicians do their best to bowl out their opponents, but they don't bomb them out. They know that they will be batting in their turn before long, and that life must not be made impossible for the man at the wicket. Even in England those who are anxious for radical reform are becoming increasingly distrustful of Parliamentary democracy. Our intellectuals profess to believe in democracy for propaganda purposes, but nobody who has studied the works of Laski, Strachey, Cole and other authors favoured by our Left Book Club, has any illusions as to the fate of democracy if these people come into power.

In England all parties are equally concerned to safeguard the framework of civilised society, but if the framework itself is imperilled, as happened in Italy and Germany, and is happening in Spain, society is sharply divided into those who wish to restore this framework, and those whose sole concern is to destroy it. When the police cease to function the average citizen is not ready to die for the abstract right to vote or freely to criticize the Government policy. These things which seem so important to us are out of the picture at times of Red peril. Ordinary people have a keen sense of the realities of life, and attach far more importance to the basic decencies of civilised life than to the right to play an infinitesimal part in the game of party politics.

Democracy in Spain has been destroyed for a generation by the extremists of the Left. Fortunately the Red Terror which provoked Franco's rising, ensured its success. Had not Franco been welcomed as a deliverer in every town where he appeared, he could never have dared that audacious and brilliant march from Algeciras to Madrid. His communications were unprotected, save that the population was on his side.

Franco to-day has some half million men on four disconnected fronts. Thousands of miles of roads leading to different parts of the front are virtually unprotected, and village after village is policed only by middle-aged volunteers wearing the scarlet beret of the Carlists or the blue forage cap of the Spanish Phalanx. On lonely mountain roads I have passed isolated and unescorted lorries. In Ireland during the Civil War no unprotected Black and Tan lorry would have reached a destination accessible only along deserted roads. If the peasantry in Nationalist Spain were hostile as the Irish peasantry were hostile, roads would be blocked by felled trees and lorries would be ambushed. But whereas the Black and Tans were fighting for a Foreign Power, Franco's army is not only National but Democratic—National because it represents the reaction against Russian dominance, Democratic because within its ranks Conservatives and Republicans, Liberals and Socialists, fight shoulder by shoulder for the reign of law and order against anarchy and chaos.

14 SHADOW ON SPAIN

Cardinal Newman distinguished between the *notional* assent to truth, the academic recognition of certain beliefs as valid, and the *real* assent inspired by personal experience. I knew before I crossed the frontier at Irun that the Reds had been guilty of wholesale atrocities, but I did not feel that Spanish horror in all its intensity until I had spent some days in Spain, days which transformed notional into real assent. The misery of those who have relations and friends behind the Red lines infect the air that one breathed. Spaniards do not tell atrocity stories. They could not retain their sanity if they allowed their minds to dwell on atrocities. They will talk of material destruction readily enough but not of spiritual tragedy.

I remember a charming and cultured man of fifty-three who had been educated at Stonyhurst and who asked eagerly after England, which he loved. I was grateful, for Spaniards to-day have little reason to love my country. I mentioned Merida, where I had just been, and he said, "I had a house there. The Reds destroyed it." And then he paused. I asked him if any of his relations had been captured by the Reds. "Well, as you ask," he said, "I'll tell you. They caught my cousin, a gallant boy of nineteen." He described in a few words how the boy was killed. It was not a nice death. And after a pause he added, "By the way, it's Boat Race day, did you know? They tell me Oxford has a good chance to win. I'll try to listen in this evening to the British wireless." And the boy who had died was never referred to again.

The shadow of evil darkens Spain to-day. It is inescapable. The Easter processions at Seville, in peace a pageant drawing thousands of tourists, have resumed their authentic penitential character. My friend's wife was walking barefoot in the procession as an act of gratitude to Our Lady because her boy had not yet been killed. A woman just behind me was describing, so my companion afterwards told me, the escape of her mother, an old woman of seventy-five, who had walked seventy miles and crossed the frontier hills at night. She had just telegraphed announcing her arrival in France. Old ladies do not do this sort of thing merely to escape from the possibility of being interned in those model prisons admired by the Duchess of Atholl during her recent visit to Spain.

In my travels I met a Spaniard in the Air Force, and he told me that parachutes had saved far more lives of airmen who had not crashed than of those who had.

"Some of our men have returned to our lines with parachutes riddled with bullets. We wear them strapped on our backs. A parachute is fine so long as you don't use it for what it is intended. I had rather crash without one than land behind the Red lines. Of course, there's always the chance of escape. One of our men pretended to be a Russian, gave the Communist salute, and wandered off without being molested; he swam a river back to our lines. Another chap who was away four days and nights crawled in with his feet cut to ribbons. The last man they caught was sorry his parachute had opened."

He added in a detached voice, "They say there's a limit

to pain, and that beyond a certain point one doesn't feel anything," and I knew that every time his engine missed a bit over the enemy lines he nerved himself with some such thought as this.

I have not quoted the story he told me because I have not been able to corroborate it. I do not know whether it was true but I know that he believed it to be true, and the belief in such things is responsible for the shadow over Spain to-day.

It is reassuring to remember that the worst atrocities were in the earlier period, and even in those days the firing squad was the normal fate of a prisoner. To-day things have so far improved that a captured officer can count with confidence on being shot.

The lower ranks have normally nothing worse to fear than imprisonment, but there are exceptions. The correspondent of the *Manchester Guardian* claims that there are many desertions in the Córdoba sector, and tells us that the deserters are sent to a base where they are cross-examined. "If they are found to be former *Guardia Civil* or members of any 'reactionary,' 'Monarchist,' or, generally speaking, 'Fascist' organisation they are shot. But if they are 'anti-Fascist,' as they nearly always are, they get a month's leave with pay and are then sent up to the line."

15 GRANADA TO MALAGA

Randolph Churchill and I left Seville after lunch on Good Friday to visit Granada and Málaga. I was glad that we had made a late start and arrived after sunset. I shall never forget the shadow of the towers of the Alhambra against the soft background of moonlit sierra snows.

I do not propose to inflict upon the reader a detailed description of the Alhambra, or even to discuss the denigration of the Spaniard at the expense of the Moor. This subject has always been popular with the sort of people who are shocked to-day that Franco should ally himself with descendants of those Moors whose contributions to Spanish culture have been so grossly exaggerated.

The Moor has magnificent qualities; he will follow to the death any leader who can command his respect, be that leader a Moor, or as in Spain to-day, a Spaniard. The true Arab is no friend of culture, he is a nomad by temperament, and culture is only possible when the nomad consents to adopt the more settled life of the agricultural community.

"If there was an Arab-Spanish civilisation," writes Louis Bertrand in his *History of Spain*, "it was especially to the Spaniards—Christians, Jews, and renegades—that this civilisation was due."

I wish that I had read *Death in the Morning* before I visited Granada. Helen Nicholson, the author, is an American by birth and has regained her American nationality after the death of her German husband. The book contains a terrible description of the incessant bombing of Granada, and the tragic story of a friend of hers who was killed by a bomb in the patio of the Hotel Washington Irving where we stayed.

> In all that scene of horror and desolation the figure . . . most clear in my mind is . . . Solita's young sister-in-law, Encarna. She was standing quite still, her face whiter than chalk, her dress splashed with blood, and a wild, fixed smile on her lips that will haunt me until I die.

That is one side of war, but there is another side.

> Those weeks of siege, when we all carried our lives in our hands, gave me something to remember, after all—something worth remembering. I think I can understand now what always used to puzzle me—why most men actually enjoy war with all its hardships and horrors, all its dangers and sordidness. Living dangerously makes life more real, more vivid, gives it a deeper meaning. And those who have lived—really lived, in this way—are not afraid to die. To some people war can be a spiritual experience.

Death in the Morning deserves to be read for many reasons. The author loves and understands the Spaniards, and interprets with great sympathy and intuition the spirit of Nationalist Spain. The book is distinguished both by beauty and by balance, and it will be read with delight by all those who love Spain.

From Granada we drove to Málaga where we lunched. Just opposite our hotel was a house burned by the Reds. Its walls were standing. A few doors further down the street was a house that had been struck by a bomb. The walls had collapsed, and little remained but the ruins.

Churchill and I paid a visit to the British Club where the ritual of the Britisher abroad was scrupulously maintained. Most of the members were playing bridge. Others were having tea.

The Málaga terror had produced its "Scarlet Pimpernel," an anarchist sickened by the excesses of his colleagues. In the new role after this revulsion of feeling he rescued many men and women from murder. He performed miracles of reckless courage, and rowed many a hunted "White" under cover of the darkness to ships out at sea.

When Málaga was captured he retired into hiding, for like St. Paul, he had been a persecutor before his conversion. A friend at the British Club asked me to do what I could to procure a guarantee for his safety if, and when, he emerged from hiding.

On my return to England I read in one of the monthly reviews that a washerwoman in Málaga had been executed by the Nationalists for the crime of washing the linen of the Reds. I wrote at once to a friend of mine who was half English, and whose mother, a British subject, lived at Málaga. I asked for news of the martyred washerwoman, and he replied, "The story is, of course, absurd. We would have warmly thanked any washerwoman who had washed not only the linen of the Reds but the Reds themselves." His mother's house had been pillaged and left in a condition of indescribable filth. It was the work of days to clean up the cathedral which stank like a sewer when the Nationalists entered the town.

For a vivid account of Málaga during the Red terror I recommend to the reader *My Fill of Days* by Sir Peter Chalmers Mitchell, whose political sympathies are with the extreme Reds. He gives an honest and objective account of the unending assassinations in Málaga during the period he describes:

"Unfortunately the Camine Nuove, well in sight of my garden, was often selected for these murders."

Sir Peter is a brave man. He sheltered several Spaniards of the Right who owe their lives to his courage. In the hectic and anarchic atmosphere of Málaga during the Terror, an Englishman, whatever his political sympathies, who protected refugees of the Right, ran grave personal risks.

On my return to Seville I heard that the Duke of Alba had arrived. One of my greatest disappointments was having just missed a visit to his historic palace in Madrid, a museum of art treasures reported in the Press to have been destroyed by an air raid, but now known to have been gutted by the Madrid forces. The Duke had invited me to lecture in Madrid, and I was on the point of leaving London when he telegraphed me to postpone my visit owing to the unsettled conditions in Spain.

I stated the case for the "Scarlet Pimpernel" and he replied that if the facts were as reported the man had nothing to fear. On the other hand, if he had alternately murdered and accepted bribes to rescue other victims, he was well advised to remain in hiding. The Duke gave me some excellent advice as to the best procedure to follow. I communicated this to my friend at Málaga with the happiest of results, for I have since heard that the "Scarlet Pimpernel" has emerged from hiding and has been granted a free pardon.

16 MEETING IN SEVILLE

I SPENT my last night in Spain with a great friend. Both at Burgos and at Salamanca I had tried to get into touch with Alvaro and failed. I was all the more overjoyed when I ran into him by accident in the Andalusia Hotel at Seville.

I first met Alvaro and his two brothers, Alonso and Ataulfo, at Mürren. Never have I known more fanatic skiers. The three brothers entered as a team representing the Kandahar Ski Club in the Parsenn-Derby, and competing against some of the finest professional racers in the world, finished second out of twelve teams. Alvaro and Alonso represented Spain in the World Ski Championship at Mürren in 1935. The Mürren kurverein welcomed them with the Spanish Republican flag, but the flag the Alcázar flew was soon raised above the hotel where Alvaro and Alonso were staying.

"Alonso and I came out to Spain together," said Alvaro, "and we read your British Ski Year Book on the journey. We often talk of the banquet after the Championship meeting, and of a remark you made in your speech . . . something to the effect that you hoped that Spain would soon expel an enemy less chivalrous and far more dangerous than the Moors."

This was in 1935. Those of us who were following events in Spain knew that the 1934 revolt of the Asturian miners was intended by Moscow as a rehearsal for a revolution.

"Alonso," continued Alvaro, "had a queer sense of impending doom on the journey to Spain. He didn't talk much, but I think he knew. The day he was killed he put his watch and his money and his other small possessions in a packet and wrapped them very carefully. He took off just after I did, and for a time we flew side by side. I waved to him, but he did not wave back. He gave me an odd look.

"Alonso was not piloting the machine; he was the observer. The weather was foul, a dense cloud and rain. Alonso's plane disappeared into the mist, and a few minutes later crashed against a mountain side."

Words seem futile when one tries to express sympathy. I was very fond of Alonso.

A few weeks after his death I was watching an international ski race with my friend Othmar Gurtner. The Italians were doing well.

"The Latins are going to beat us all at ski-ing," said Gurtner, "just as they do in motor racing. Their timing is better. Do you remember Alonso?"

I knew what he meant. Alonso had the Latin recklessness. With a little more training he might have been a world beater.

Alvaro spoke very warmly of the Italian flyers. Their machines were not as good as the Russians', but they brought down more planes than any airmen on either side.

We dined together, and towards midnight I went up to my room and Alvaro came with me. He threw open the window, and we could hear an aeroplane approaching. There was a low ceiling of cloud, and the pilot was trying to land. The aerodrome was sending up rockets, but they scarcely penetrated through the clouds. Again and again the aeroplane circled round and then again retreated.

"Ataulfo may be in that aeroplane," said Alvaro

anxiously. "Poor devil! I know just what the pilot's feeling. He can't see a damned thing, and he's cursing the aerodrome for not showing more lights."

Once again the aeroplane approached.

"I hope he makes it," said Alvaro. "He's having a shot at it. He's coming down. Good. He's landed."

The charm of my society was not what kept Alvaro in my room until two in the morning. It was that I represented a link with the things he loved, with the clean battles of the snows, with the mountains . . . with peace. And when he turned to say good-bye I felt a sense of humiliating dereliction. He was returning to the front, and I was going back to England, to comfort and to security.

17 JOURNEY'S END

B<small>EFORE LEAVING</small> for England, I spent a day in Gibraltar. I called on the Roman Catholic Bishop of Gibraltar. Refugees have been pouring into Gibraltar from Spain and he had been close to the Spanish tragedy.

"Only yesterday we received a party of nuns that had escaped on a British battleship. I assure you, Mr. Lunn, I have dined every night with horrors. But when I spoke of these things to some of my Anglican friends who were having tea with me the other day, they dismissed them all as 'mere propaganda.' I only wish I could agree with them."

I am writing these lines in the early morning, and a persistent thrush has deflected my attention from my typewriter. Through the open windows I have just glanced at the roses in our garden. It is all very beautiful, and yet this tranquil loveliness is curiously unsatisfying. My feelings are disconcertingly like Helen Nicholson's on her return to England:

> But in spite of this comfortable feeling of security, I was already homesick for Granada, as I have been ever since. Even after Asta and Alfonso joined me, months later, this ache of longing persisted, and I have walked along Piccadilly in the

December gloom and mist, seeing only a beleaguered, sunbaked town, with the high mountains standing all about, secret and fateful; and the gay legionaries lounging in the cafés, or swinging along the streets in pairs. At times, in some crowded room, a whiff of perfume has brought back the scented, starlit nights, with the lorries full of tired soldiers rattling through the town after a battle, crying: 'Viva España!'

Nostalgia takes many forms. I never see the spire of Harrow church without remembering the desolation of the return to Harrow from the mountains. And there is a street in a middle-western town always associated in my mind with an evening when I emerged from an Italian film with memories of Romanesque campaniles set against the immensities of Maggiore's blue.

The longing for the Alps and for Italy is more tolerable than the nostalgia for wartime Spain. I shall enjoy England again when peace returns; I am only conscious of the contrast between the soporific security of the English air and the austere climate of heroic Spain, a climate which impressed me first when I crossed the international bridge at Hendaye. I had nothing to declare but my love for Spain when I entered the Customs at Irún, and I had nothing to surrender save my heart as I passed the frontier guards at Algeciras. One day I shall return and claim it.

"Heroic Spain." How this phrase will grate upon those who insist that our supreme concern in life must be to pass through life as comfortably and as painlessly as possible. Praise of physical courage is distasteful to a certain kind of pacifist, but it is not necessary to sacrifice truth on the altar of peace or to belittle heroism merely because one believes that the evils of war outweigh its redeeming features. Nor will pacifists of this school—and there are other schools—ever succeed in destroying respect for military virtue which is as old as man and will endure so long as man endures. This particular form of pacifism is the mood of a passing moment and already a little dated. The Immortals never date, and Shakespeare speaks to our age no less than to his in the closing scene of *Macbeth*.

Ross.	Your son, my lord, has paid a soldier's debt:
	He only lived but till he was a man;
	The which no sooner had his prowess confirm'd.
	In the unshrinking station where he fought,
	But like a man he died.
Siward.	Then he is dead?
Ross.	Ay, and brought off the field: your cause of sorrow
	Must not be measured by his worth, for then
	It hath no end.
Siward.	Had he his hurts before?
Ross.	Ay, on the front.
Siward.	Why then, God's soldier be he!
	Had I as many sons as I have hairs,
	I would not wish them to a fairer death.

There are many Siwards in Nationalist Spain, parents whose stoic acceptance of sacrifice is as impressive as the courage of their sons in the front rank. Characteristic of this spirit is the well-known story of the Carlist widow of whose three sons two enlisted in the first hour of the war. The third, a boy of sixteen, not unnaturally assumed that he was too young. That evening when he came down to supper he saw that only one place had been laid. "I don't lay places for cowards," said his mother. The boy enlisted next day.

It was men born of such mothers that held the Alcázar and continued to hold the Alcázar long after the world believed them to be doomed. "Thinkest thou that all my suns are set?" That was their answer to the world, an answer anticipated long ago by Theocritus, for Theocritus, like Shakespeare, interprets not the mood of a moment, but the enduring things even "Progress" cannot wholly destroy.

The thrush has stopped singing, and distant echoes of *¡Arriba España!* come to me on breezes of memory. My mind eludes the officials of the Non-Intervention Committee and I am back again in a little garden at Pozuelo among flower beds where violets dispute the desolation of war. I see the deep gorge of the Tagus and women in mourning praying in Seville Cathedral, and the sweep of Spanish hills, and the towers of the Alhambra silhouetted against moonlit snows, and young men going up into the line, and the sadness in the eyes of those whose sons will not return.

They will tell you many things, these Spaniards whom you meet behind the lines, but they cannot tell the ultimate secret, for, as Henry James somewhere says, "Things which involve risk are like the Christian faith. They must be seen from the inside."

PART II

1 THE USE AND ABUSE OF LABELS

Happy is the man who knows the value of research.
                                                Euripides.

I WAS RECENTLY ASKED to talk to a group of undergraduates at the University of London. In the course of my remarks I quoted from Andrew Smith's book *I Was a Soviet Worker*. Smith was a convinced Communist who gave his life savings to the Communist Party and set sail from America for the Promised Land. After working for three years in Soviet Russia he returned to tell his fellow Communists that Russia treats her workers worse than Capitalist countries treat their dogs.

When I had finished, a young Communist arose and put a question.

"Are you aware," he asked, "that Smith is a Trotskyite?"

I asked him if he could produce any evidence in support of this theory. He could produce no evidence. Smith, he implied, must be a Trotskyite because he had dared to criticize Soviet Russia.

I suggested that the point at issue was not whether Smith was a Trotskyite but whether Smith's statements could be disproved. This shocked him.

A subsequent speaker made an interesting point weakening the force of my argument and illustrating the fact that a lecturer who invites questions seldom leaves the lecture hall without acquiring information. As I came out of the room I found the young Communist indignantly denouncing my bourgeois ideology to a group of friends. He snarled at me as I approached and said, "Anyhow, that man at the back of the hall stumped you with his question."

Why "stumped?" The man at the back of the hall had told me something I did not know. I cannot see why I should resent acquiring information. At forty-nine one is, of course, less perturbed than at twenty-two by the discovery that one is not infallible, and more grateful to those who add to one's small store of knowledge. I tried to explain this but without effect.

This young Communist was characteristic of an age, when flight from reason is developing into a rout. He was not interested in truth unless truth could be exploited in the interests of Communism. Facts were of value only as they fitted into his own particular creed.

In the concluding paragraphs of that entertaining book, *The Testament of Joad,* C. E. M. Joad satirizes not only himself but the prevailing tendency of this age exemplified by my young Communist friend in his attitude. After analysing the Rhine experiments in telepathy Mr. Joad explains that the new facts discovered by Rhine fit very conveniently into the Joadian philosophy.

"The fit is perfect, but then if they had not fitted I should not have been disposed to attach much importance to them."

The literal translation of the Greek word *zetesis* is "seeking," and a philosophy of life is crystallized in this word, that eager curiosity characteristically Hellenic. There is little of this Greek spirit in the modern world. Slogans and labels are our modern substitutes for intellectual curiosity. Smith is a Trotskyite. So much for

Smith. No need to read his book or to meet his arguments. Russian "Smiths" are put down by bullets, American Smiths, by labels. Words should stimulate thought, but are degenerating into labels to save people the necessity of thinking; no word is more useful for this soporific purpose than "Fascist."

If you object to dictatorship in Russia you are a Fascist. If you criticize certain aspects of democracy in England you are a Fascist. If you disapprove of that régime of terror following the institution of the Popular Front in Spain, you are a Fascist. If you hope for friendlier relations with Italy, if you resent the mischievous activities of our pacifist warmongers, if you are not prepared for your son to die for Geneva, you are a Fascist.

And if you are a Fascist nobody need bother any further with your views or your arguments.

Perhaps the most popular thought-saving labels are the words "progressive" and "reactionary." If I have taken the wrong turning, figuratively speaking, it is foolish to progress any further in the wrong direction. On the contrary, I should react towards the crossroads where I went wrong.

Labels are valuable if they help to clarify thought, pernicious if they are accepted as substitutes for thought. To fix such labels as "Fascist," "Communist," or "Democratic" over the map of Europe is a waste of time. Never has Europe been more interesting to those who make some effort to understand the springs of political action. Intellectual curiosity induces happiness, intellectual incuriosity, boredom. Russia, Italy and Germany are laboratories for experiments which will change the face of the world, and few of those who talk so glibly of Fascism or Communism seem concerned to discover what those experiments are.

I do not know which is the more tiresome, uncritical abuse of Communism by rich people who fear, and are right to fear, that Communism will make them poorer, or the uncritical praise of Communism by the poor who believe, and who are mistaken in believing, that Communism will make them richer. Among those who are noisiest in their denunciation of Communism or loudest in their praise, how few have read Marx, and how few could, if challenged, give a summary of what Marx meant by dialectical materialism. Surely, some knowledge of the philosophy, economics and history of Communism should be regarded as an integral part of modern education. Communism is responsible for some absorbingly interesting literature, ranging from the theoretical appreciations and criticisms by writers such as Strachey and Dawson, Laski and Berdyaev, Trotsky and Gurian, to accounts of first-hand experience from authors such as Hindus, Andrew Smith, Pares, Lyall, Wicksteed, Delafield and many others.

Communism owes its vitality to its gospel of deliverance for the dispossessed. "Thou hast put down the mighty from their seats and hast exalted the humble and meek." Those words have crystallized the inspiration behind all revolutions, and certainly Communism in its earlier phases professed to give a new dignity and a new status to the common man. But even those who believe, as I do, that Russia to-day is governed by a clique of terrified terrorists, and that the lot of the common man is far worse in modern Russia than in Czarist Russia, are not absolved by this belief from the intellectual duty of attempting to understand one of the most interesting experiments in the modern world. Russia, as Professor Laski somewhere remarks, is the most exciting country in modern Europe, so exciting that Professor Laski is well advised to stay where he is.

Russia is not the only country conducting experiments. Germany has something to teach us, and yet when our Ambassador in Berlin hinted in his inaugural speech that he had something to learn from Germany, our provincial

Labourites exploded with noisy indignation; they repudiated with scorn the suggestion that "our great democracy" had anything to learn from dictators, excepting only Russian dictators.

No word is more abused in the modern world than democracy"; it is a soothing incantation for those who tacitly assume that democracy needs no definition. The literal meaning of the word is "power of the people," and this does not take us very far. If a Government is democratic merely because it rests on "the power of the people," and enjoys the support of the majority of its citizens, Italian Fascism is democratic whereas the Spanish Popular Front never was. Mussolini, as an anti-Fascist Italian sadly remarked to me, still commands the confidence of the overwhelming majority of Italians; the Spanish Popular Front polled nearly half a million less votes at the elections than the Opposition.

If democracy means the government of the people by the people for the people, Periclean Athens was democratic if you accept the Athenian view that neither women nor slaves should play a part in public affairs. The Athenian citizen did not elect a legislator to represent him, but voted in person on all political and financial measures. Great Britain, on the other hand, is not governed *by* the people but by *representatives of the people,* a very different matter. In Latin countries democracy is too often government of the people by the politicians for the politicians.

Democracy need not necessarily mean Parliamentary Government on a territorial basis, for a democratic Parliament might be elected not only by counties and by boroughs but by professions and trades. Whatever our definition of democracy, nothing could be more fatuous than to assume that a majority has a divine right to do precisely what it pleases. *The success of democratic government depends far less on the machinery of election than on how the elected interpret their mandate, and the respect shown by the majority for the rights of the minority.*

Democracy has been a success in Great Britain because British democracy is permeated with the spirit of fair play. The recent proposal to pay the Leader of the Opposition £2,000 a year does not seem unreasonable to those who believe that the success of the Parliamentary system depends on an effective and critical opposition. Under the rule of the Popular Front in Spain, members of the Opposition were threatened with assassination, and their leader was murdered by the police. *Where respect for minorities disappears, democracy is doomed,* as that great democrat, Abraham Lincoln, fully realized. "Our progress in degeneracy," he said, "appears to be pretty rapid. As a nation we began by declaring that all men are created equal except negroes. When the know-nothings get control, it will read all men are created equal, except negroes and foreigners and Catholics. When it comes to this, I shall prefer emigration to some country where they make no pretence of loving liberty—to Russia, for instance, where despotism can be taken pure, without the base alloy of hypocrisy."

> That is the position to-day [Mr. Arthur Bryant in *The Observer*] of many Spanish Liberals now fighting for Franco, who found that the practical interpretation of Spanish democracy involved the denial of liberty to all but Communists and Anarchists. In Red Spain to-day minorities have no rights—not even to exist.
>
> To demand a crusade in the name of democracy to defend the rights of a Spanish faction to annihilate its opponents is to bring real democracy into ridicule. Even if that faction represented a majority of the Spanish people, which it does not, a constitutional country like Britain can have no interest in defending cruelty or crime. A brutal act is not made any the more excusable because it is committed by a majority. To allege that it is, is to claim the same kind of divinity for a mob as used to be claimed for Kings, and in several countries to-day—including Soviet Russia—is claimed for dictators.

Democracy is not the divine right of Kings standing on its head.

I know there are many who believe that, because such a country as Spain was misgoverned in the past, the reign of terror that has rendered that part of it subject to the so-called rule of Valencia a shambles does not matter. It is merely, so it is argued, a passing phase. The burning of a nun in petrol or the sawing off of a Conservative tradesman's legs—the commonplaces of 'democratic' Spain for many blood-stained months—are merely the high-spirited antics of a young and exuberant democracy; the first fine careless rapture of a popular crusade for freedom; a necessary stage in the course of evolutionary progress.

But however trivial these excesses may seem in the cold detachment of the philosopher's study in the security of an ordered land where such things are impossible, their effect in practice is not to advance the evolution of a nation towards democracy but to retard it. For, leaving aside the sickening cruelty and suffering involved in the Marxian 'blood-bath,' its result, as has been proved in every Western community where it has been applied, is to provoke a violent reaction against everything that in time might create a real democracy. Faced by the despotism of the local mob—of all that is basest and most degraded in human nature and society—the ordinary, decent citizen surrenders his legitimate freedom in despair to the first strong man who is able to restore public order. Anarchy, which our short-sighted publicists of the unthinking Left have invested with the great and honourable name of democracy, is the rock on which the very idea of democracy shipwrecks.

2 AN OUTLINE OF COMMUNIST TACTICS

MADRID TO-DAY,[1] according to *The Times* correspondent, is the biggest experiment that "Communism has ever raised in the West." And the correspondent might have added that the Spanish War is necessarily incomprehensible to those who have never studied Communist methods and tactics in Soviet Russia.

Space permits only the briefest outline of Communist methods, but some such outline is essential for an understanding of the Spanish War. This chapter is intended to serve not as a substitute for, but as a stimulant to research, for Communism thrives on the apathy and indifference of those who have most to fear from a Red revolution.

Red is a fashionable colour in modern England. It is easier to refute arguments than to fight fashion, but all those who are determined that the Spanish tragedy shall not be re-enacted in England are under an obligation to study Communism and to arm themselves with the facts that refute Red fictions. Communists are creating cells in every

[1] November 21, 1936.

regiment, trade, club and university, and unless we are equally active and equally alert, their ambitions may be realised.

I was recently challenged, as I have remarked elsewhere in this book, by the Birkenhead Communists to meet their champion in debate. I accepted the challenge subject to the proviso that their champion should be accredited by the Communist Party of Great Britain as a representative competent to defend their policy on the public platform. I was not in the least surprised to learn that this proviso was not acceptable. The chiefs of the British Communist Party are wiser than the rank and file. They know that it is impossible for a Communist to emerge with success from a debate in which he dare not defend, and cannot disavow, the official policy of his Party. Communism is rotten with intellectual dishonesty, for Communists are instructed to preach, for tactical reasons, a policy they will disavow when the moment comes to strike. They preach peace while preparing for war.

"The Communist Party of Great Britain," to quote from its Rules, "is a section of the Communist International and is bound by its decisions." The point is important, for British Communists often attempt to suggest that British Communism is very different from the Russian model.

Every British Communist is the agent of a foreign power whose avowed and declared object is the fomenting of civil strife. It is the duty of British Communists to form revolutionary cells in every regiment and in every unit of the Fleet. The Communists insist that revolution is impossible unless the armed forces can be persuaded to join the workers in revolt. In London, March 1933, at an anti-War Conference, attended by representatives of twenty-four societies, the delegates were informed that the procedure in the event of war was to not strike but for the workers to take the rifles thrust into their hands and turn them upon their officers.

Terrorism is the official policy of the Communists in the

penultimate phase before the outbreak of revolution, as for instance during the Red terror in Spain under the Popular Front, during the time the Revolutionary Government is consolidating its power. Lenin, in the course of drafting the Soviet Penal Code, declared that "the legal trial is not intended to replace terrorism . . . but to base terrorism firmly on a fundamental principle."[1]

Mr. Walter Duranty, who affects an attitude of genial neutrality so far as Communism is concerned, obtained a copy of an official treatise on Terrorism, and in his book *I Write As I Please*,[2] he summarizes the principles defined in this treatise. "Action must be ruthless and above all swift. . . . Secrecy was also stressed because that, too, was an element of terror."

On the night of the attempt on Lenin's life, five hundred people were executed without trial, not because they were involved in the plot, but because they were class enemies whose execution would terrorize enemies of the Soviet régime. Mr. Duranty quotes from a history of the Communist Party by Popov. "The system of mass Red terror proved a weapon of tremendous importance." It did in Spain no less than in Russia.

A striking illustration of mass Red terror was the deliberate extirpation of the recalcitrant peasants of the Ukraine. "Obsolete classes," Stalin told H. G. Wells, "do not voluntarily disappear." When the peasants resisted collective farming he sent Government grain collectors to seize the small share of the crops saved for their own use. By this act he condemned millions to death as surely as if he had condemned them to be shot. The number of peasants who died of starvation has been estimated by W. H. Chamberlin (*Russia's Iron Age*) at five million.

There is one easy method of reducing Communist hecklers to sulky silence. Ask them if they are prepared to

---
[1] Quoted in *The Bolshevik*, October 31, 1930.
[2] Page 187.

defend capital punishment for children. The death penalty was abolished for a brief period at the beginning of the Revolution; the qualifying age for the now restored death penalty has been lowered to twelve, and theft is included among capital offences.

Max Eastman, an old Marxian Communist, contributed to *Harper's Magazine* in February 1937 an article on *The End of Socialism in Russia*; he writes: "In the spring of 1935 Stalin's government issued a decree which made the death penalty for theft—adopted for adults three years before—applicable to minors from the age of twelve. When this fact was announced at a congress of the French Teachers' Federation in August of the same year, the Stalinists in the Federation indignantly denied it. Being shown a copy of *Izvestia*[1] containing the decree, they lapsed into silence, but they were ready next day with information that 'under socialism children are so precocious and well educated that they are fully responsible for their acts'! It is a reflection of how this ideology is being stretched to cover every saddest thing in Russia."

Is it surprising that the Birkenhead Communists were not encouraged to debate? British Communists have been sadly worried by the wholesale liquidation of the old Bolshevik guard. A young man in a Communist bookshop who mistook me for a sympathizer because I bought some Communist pamphlets remarked sadly, "These Russians make things so difficult for us." They do indeed.

"The list of those shot," writes Max Eastman, "or who shot themselves, or who were named as implicated with the victims comprises—with a single exception—every one of the eminent Bolsheviks who sat with Stalin around the council-table of Lenin:[2] Trotsky, Zinoviev, Kamenev,

[1] April 8, 1935.
[2] "The exception is Rakovsky, whose distinction is that he was the last of all to give up open opposition, and capitulate to Stalin's dictatorship, remaining in exile until 1933, and capitulating all too obviously in a sick if not a senile despair."

Rykov, Bukharin, Radek, Sokolnikov, Piatakov (mentioned in Lenin's Testament as among the ablest), Yevdokimov, Smirnov (once known as 'The Lenin of Siberia'), Tomsky (head of the Federation of Labour), Serebriakov (Stalin's predecessor as secretary of the party), and several others only a little less eminent."

There was only one Judas among the twelve apostles, but if Stalin is to be believed, there were ten Judases among the first twelve apostles of Communism. If St. Peter had killed as a traitor to Christianity every Apostle save one, it is probable that Christianity would not have survived.

It is not only human beings who have been destroyed. The traditional culture of Christian Europe is regarded with venomous hatred by the Communists, and the intellectuals associated with that culture have been persecuted as ruthlessly as the rich and the aristocratic.

International culture, the ideals of humanism, freedom of thought and freedom for research, have been betrayed by our Left-Wing intellectuals. They have been ready enough to protest against oppression in Germany and Italy, but their sense of international unity has disappeared in face of the persecution in Soviet Russia. With a few honourable exceptions these leftist individuals remain silent, and condone by their silence the ruthless onslaught upon the intellectual life of a great people

"To wipe out the intellectuals as a class," writes the author of *I Escape from the Soviet*, the wife of a distinguished Russian Scientist, Tchernavin, "it was necessary to get hold of not only the men, but the women as well, and their children."

In a letter to *The Times* on April 24, 1933, Sir Bernard Pares, Professor of Russian at the University of London, wrote as follows: "There is no doubt whatever as to the accuracy of Professor Tchernavin's account of his treatment in Russian prisons. He is a distinguished ichthyologist, and has been able to supply us with details as to the fate of numerous scholars, of whom we had lost track;

some of them are known to me, and some have European reputations. Of fifty-one he knew in his own branch of science, twenty-five have been shot and twenty-six deported in three years (1930–1932). Among those whom he knew personally or met in prison his list includes six academicians and thirty-six in other professions in various fields or custodians of museums."

Every culture is the product of a philosophy. The culture of Christian Europe is the expression of the Christian belief in the infinite value of every human soul. "Proletculture" is the expression of Marxian materialism, the doctrine that there is no qualitative difference between men and machines, a doctrine which leads to the conclusion that the individual is an unimportant cog in the machinery of the state.

"The reading books for the children are mechanized, and are designed to fix the child's attention on representations of technical objects; there are no pictures of flowers, animals, or such 'bourgeois idyllic' things. The mind of the child is to be directed to machinery. 'Processions of children,' wrote a visitor to Russia in October 1931, 'are seen marching with banners bearing inscriptions such as "Give us technical power!"'"[1]

Communism wages war on three fronts: economic, religious and cultural. "In 1926 the Communist authorities sent urgent instructions to one hundred and twenty libraries in Leningrad to destroy all volumes of *belles-lettres* (dating before 1917) out of harmony with Communist doctrine."[2]

The destruction of the magnificent Oviedo Library in Spain in the course of the 1934 rebellion which the Communists subsidized with money and arms, was not a spontaneous act of unplanned violence, but a characteristic incident in the war between proletculture and European culture.

---

[1] *The Communist Attack on Great Britain* by G. M. Godden, p. 62.
[2] *Ibid.*, p. 63.

W. H. Chamberlin in *Russia's Iron Age* states that "Soviet intellectual life has been very much under the influence of two slogans: 'Art on the Class Front,' and the *'partiinost'* (Party character) of science. . . . A journal entitled *For Marxist-Leninist Natural Science* blossomed forth with such slogans as 'For Party Spirit in Mathematics,' and 'For Purity of Marxist-Leninist Theory in Surgery.'"

André Gide, once a Communist, has described in *Return from the U.S.S.R.* the destruction of culture in Russia. "I doubt," he writes, "if in any other country to-day, such as Germany under Hitler, the spirit is less free, more terrorized."

Proletculture wages relentless war on religion. Moscow is very clever in adapting its atheistic propaganda to the ideological level of the people whom it wishes to convert. Though the attack on the traditional Christian morality is still concealed, the attack on the Christian creed is daily becoming less timid. Early in 1932 the University of London Union lent its Hall for an exhibition of Soviet Education, including Exhibits of five stages in the training of children in atheism. One of the exhibits was a caricature of the Deity "inscribed with the word 'God' so that there should be no mistake, with which hardly a printer in the world, outside the Union of Soviet and Socialist Republics, would foul his printing press."[1]

The ephemeral success of Communism in Germany and in Italy created Fascism. Communism was defeated in Hungary, and left nothing behind save the memory of the Red terror. Outside Russia Communism failed completely, though a doubtful exception might perhaps be made for Mexico.

The Seventh Annual Congress of the Third International held in Moscow during July and August 1935 realised that the methods which had failed so signally would need to be

[1] Godden: *op. cit.*, p. 49.

revised. This Congress was described by Georgi Dimitrov as "the new tactical approach."

It was decided that the propaganda of terrorism should be held in reserve during the period of preparation for open revolution. Communists were to be encouraged to insinuate themselves into Christian Churches, Peace societies, athletic associations and youth movements.

The following quotations from the Revolutionary programme are significant. "Where there is no revolutionary upsurge, the Communist Party must advance by partial slogans." Again, "Outline non-revolutionary methods to win youth and take them over in Bolshevik fashion."

The policy of the Communist penumbra has developed with considerable success in the years following the Seventh Congress. The Communist penumbra comprises Socialists or advanced Radicals who are not members of the Communist Party, and who therefore provoke far less hostility than avowed Communists. A rapid increase in the numbers of the Communist Party is liable to provoke a Fascist reaction. The Communists, therefore, aim at creating a Communist nucleus surrounded by sympathetic allies who describe themselves as Socialists or Radicals. Their technique has proved of the greatest value to Spain, and has enabled many supporters of the Valencia Government to deceive, perhaps themselves, and certainly public opinion, by the pretence that the strength of Spanish Communism may be measured by the number of its declared supporters. Lenin in his instructions for the founding of a Communist paper declared "We must, in the beginning, be very prudent. The paper must not be too revolutionary, in the beginning. If you have three editors, at least one must be a non-Communist."[1]

The Daily Worker is an admirable example of overt undisguised propaganda. It is the official organ of British

[1] *Lenin on Britain*, 1934, p. 272.

Communism, but perhaps less effective as propaganda than the numerous trade papers of the Communist penumbra. Among these papers and cyclostyle sheets: *Power*, the paper for electrical workers, *The Red Letter* for postal workers, *The Working Baker*, *The Furniture Worker*, *The Jogger* for clerks, *The Busman's Punch*, *The Railway Vigilant*, *The London Docker*, *The Seafarer*, etc. These papers are Communist in tendency, but they avoid the symbols of the workers' revolutionary Government, the hammer and sickle, and seldom contain open incitement to revolt.

Far the most successful invention of the Communist Party is the "Popular Front," compared by Dimitrov to the Trojan Horse, because it conceals the invaders until they are *inside* ready to capture the citadel of Democracy.

Fascism is intensely unpopular in the English-speaking world, in the United States no less than in Great Britain. Communists are instructed therefore to represent themselves as the supporters of democracy. Because the fear of war is universal, Communists must pose as the friends of peace. Communists are the driving force behind "The League Against Fascism and War," its aim to enroll all anti-Fascists and pacifists. The League could more properly be described as a league to *promote* Communism and Civil War. At the Amsterdam Anti-War Congress in 1932 the French Communist leader Marcel Cachen said, "You ask for our tactics. These are our tactics. Transforming imperialist war into civil war."[1]

"Collective security" means security for Russia to prepare "collective insecurity" for Great Britain and France. Realists in these matters are the Swiss, who have discovered that Litvinoff's slogan "Peace is indivisible" is being exploited to prepare for that "indivisible war," and Europe may be involved very soon. If there be a country

[1] *Daily Worker*, August 30, 1932.

which has no aggressive designs against its neighbours; has everything to lose and nothing to gain from war; has consistently welcomed every Peace conference, and lavished hospitality on the prophets of Peace—that country is Switzerland. Why then did Switzerland decide at the eleventh hour to cancel her permission for the Anti-War Congress to meet at Geneva, so that in consequence the Congress ultimately met in Brussels? Because the Swiss had come to the conclusion that these Congresses are exploited by Communists to promote, not peace, but war. The enemies of Mussolini and Hitler despair of a successful revolution from within, and are turning their thoughts to the possibilities a European war might provide for overthrowing Fascism from without. Such were the reasons given in the influential Swiss paper, *Neue Zürcher Zeitung* of Zürich for a decision appearing on the surface to be the reverse of the traditional policy of the Swiss Confederation.

In conclusion I cannot stress too strongly the danger of equating Communism with Russian Communism. Communism is collapsing in Russia, but it is being *reborn* in that Fourth International which accepts Trotsky as its leader. And this Fourth International will wage a war as ruthless as its predecessor on the tradition and values of Christian civilization.

Meanwhile our own situation is precarious. *Many of those to whom we entrust the education of our young are Left-Wing in their sympathy.* Many of them are avowed Communists. The attack on the Christian creed, the foundation of that Christian culture which made England great, is proceeding unchecked in Board Schools, Elementary Schools and in the Universities. Unless the present tendency can be arrested the fruits of a false philosophy will prove to be no less bitter in this country than in Russia and in Spain.

3 COMMUNIST PREPARATIONS IN SPAIN, 1869-1932

LET ME BEGIN by drawing a distinction between different forms of national propaganda. Propaganda may be designed to influence the foreign policy of a state, and to ensure an alliance if possible, or at least the benevolent neutrality of the state, in the event of war. Diplomatic propaganda conducted by the great powers in Turkey and in the Balkans before the war were similar to most of the activities described in this book. In the event of a war between Germany and France, the attitude of Spain would be important, but it is difficult to understand why it should be more sinister for Germany than for France to desire the success of the political party in Spain most favourably disposed towards her.

Russian propaganda not only seeks to influence the policy of friendly states in its favour, and to secure their alliance in time of war, but to provoke civil war within the borders of the state. Russia hopes by civil war to transform foreign countries into units of that Soviet union of republics whose frontiers in the utopian vision of Marx are conterminous with the limits of the habitable globe. For tactical reasons Stalin professes to have abandoned all hope of world revolution, but we are concerned in this chapter, not with his present profession, but with the past effects of the Soviet policy never really revised.

The Germans are accused in this book of Nazi propaganda among the Arabs of French Morocco. If this charge could be proved, the Nazis would stand convicted of an act unfriendly to France; the case against them in Spain would remain to be proved. Admittedly the Italians and the Germans helped Franco from the outset of the war, but there is no evidence in this book that they had long plotted a Fascist rising, or that the rising itself had been planned by Franco many weeks before the opening of hostilities. What is certain is that Russian intervention in Spain antedates by many years this alleged Nazi conspiracy Only a propagandist writing for the ignorant could pretend that peaceful democracy was the victim of an unprovoked Fascist attack. The well-informed correspondent of the *Manchester Guardian* has no such illusions. "In a formal sense," he writes, "the rebellion started the civil war, but in a real sense it is very uncertain what came first, revolution or rebellion. The rebellion certainly opened the civil war and precipitated full revolution. Whether there would have been full revolution if there had been no open rebellion is a question which has no final answer."[1]

Spanish Marxism dates from 1869 when a Marxist Manifesto was issued by the Madrid Section; Spanish Marxists were organized as autoritarios in 1870. During the revolution of 1873 the Spanish Marxists exploited opportunities for loot and arson. Emilio Castelar, one of the founders of the first republic, described the results of that luckless revolutionary experiment. "Daily riots, general strife and military indiscipline have been let loose everywhere. Our colleagues are being killed in the streets

[1] July 1, 1937.

of towns that a short time ago were peaceful. . . . We have arson and murder at Alcoy, anarchy at Valencia, and brigandage in Sierra Morena. Murcia is in the hands of the demagogues and Castellón has fallen to the reactionaries. . . . The Spanish fleet alternately hoists a red flag and a foreign banner."

In 1909 Spain suffered from a period of Syndicalist terrorism. Thirty-six churches were burned in Barcelona, railways were torn up and electrical and gas works were destroyed. In 1917 a revolutionary General Strike spread over Spain; a state of war was declared, and machine-guns swept the barricaded streets of Madrid and Barcelona. From 1919 to 1920 the fear of terrorists was so great that "it was practically impossible to obtain a verdict of guilty in any of the many trials for murder and manslaughter."[1] In 1920 the Spanish section of the Stalin party comprised 800 members. By April 1932 the membership had increased to 12,000, and the first "Youth Cell" had no less than 8,000 members.

The first outstanding triumph of Communist propaganda was the revolution resulting in the abdication of King Alfonso XIII, who left after the Municipal Elections. Four-fifths of Spain had voted Monarchist, and Sir George Young, whose book *The New Spain* is the best study of Republican Spain by a writer of extreme Left-Wing views, writes, "If you ask why a reigning house and a ruling class should renounce the power they had held for time out of mind because Municipal Elections had given them a majority of only four to one, why, I can only refer you to previous pages for proof that in Spanish democracy you need not trouble to count noses to learn when the noes have it."

---

[1] *Spain To-day* by F. B. Deakin. Labour Publishing Co., pp. 96–97.

4 THE RED TAIL THAT WAGGED THE PINK DOG

Directly the King left, the Red tail began to wag the pink dog. Churches were burnt, sculpture and paintings were destroyed in that iconoclastic fury incited by Moscow. Constitutional guarantees were suppressed, and the freedom of the Press restricted at every turn.

What was the reaction of our Liberal Press to these attacks on Liberalism as it was once understood? Did they protest in the name of democratic government against these abuses of democracy, or in the name of religious freedom against religious persecution? They remained silent.

Within a year of the establishment of the Republic a cautious *Times* correspondent reported in a message from Madrid that "evidence continues to accumulate that the Spanish Republic is being made the victim of a vast conspiracy against law and order . . . in the background there is reason to believe the existence of clandestine and powerful forces."[1]

In October 1932 the *Communist International* announced

---

[1] *The Times*, June 2, 1932.

that "Revolution is taking place in Spain, and at the present time the mass movement is seething and showing tendencies to develop into an armed revolt of the people."

On January 11, 1933, *The Times* correspondent wrote from Barcelona: "One of the outstanding leaders of the Communist movement here is Andres Nin, a Catalán, who was in Moscow as one of Trotsky's chief lieutenants when Trotsky was in power there, and who has been his confidential agent here, preparing the groundwork for the possible triumph of Communism. In a recent statement to your correspondent Nin gave a clue to the working of the minds of all those bent upon bringing about a social revolution. He said: 'We began first with an educational campaign, and now we are engaged in organizing Workers' Soviets in anticipation of the crucial moment when the Workers must be the first to arrive on the scene and to seize power . . . we undertook to group the masses round the symbols of democracy, such symbols as they could understand, to give the masses illusions . . . we organized political juntas, which in Spain have a traditional significance, and *which at the right moment could be converted into Soviets.*'"

In September the first step towards a Popular Front was formed by the united front of Socialists and Communists. At a meeting in Madrid representatives of *both* parties "announced that only a Marxist régime would satisfy them."[1]

All informed students of Communism are aware that the policy of Moscow is to exploit not only the small nucleus of official Communists in such countries as Spain, but the large penumbra of Communist allies masquerading for tactical purposes under other names. The virtual identity of Socialists and Communists in Spain is proved by the declaration I have just quoted.

---

[1] *The Times*, September 17, 1934.

Francisco Largo Caballero, Prime Minister of the Valencia Government at the beginning of the year, has never been an official Communist, but he takes his orders from Moscow, and this was his New Year's message to Soviet Russia: "The proletariat of Iberia will try to follow the example of your great country."

In October 1933 the General Election had resulted in the return of a Cortes in which the Right Wing and Centre controlled the majority. Within a year the Reds, who were in a minority, had risen in armed rebellion. The rebellion was quickly suppressed in Madrid, but in the Asturias the rebels were overcome only with considerable difficulty. Our liberal press, so disedified by the fact that the Nationalists have resorted to arms in their attempt to overthrow the Popular Front, was no less shocked by the determination of the Government in 1934 to suppress a rebellion.

Before the revolution broke out "opinion was genuinely alarmed when it was announced that a consignment of seventy cases of arms had been landed in Asturias."[1] In October 1934 the "first Soviet Republic in Spain" was established in the Asturias under that name, and the currency circulated by the rebels was stamped with the sickle and hammer.[2] The organ of the Communist International summed up the civil war in the Asturias in these words: "The Workers of Asturias fought for Soviet Power under the leadership of the Communists."[3]

In 1934, two years before a German or Italian aeroplane appeared in Spain, and two years before any Italian or German volunteer landed on Spanish soil, Russia intervened in Spain by inciting a rebellion against the

---

[1] *The Spanish Tragedy* by E. Allison Peers, p. 159.
[2] *Spain*, October, 1934. S.R.I., Paris.
[3] The Communist International, November 5, 1934, English edition, p. 807.

Republican Government. At the same time the British Reds who have since protested so violently against German and Italian intervention, expressed their strong sympathy, not with the forces of order, but with those who had appealed to arms against the constitutionally-elected Government.

During the course of the rebellion, characteristic acts of Communist vandalism resulted in the destruction of the world famous Cámara Santo (Bishop's Palace) and the 40,000 volumes of the Oviedo University Library. Twenty-seven priests were murdered and one was burned alive. Left-Wing intellectuals who were so distressed by the destruction of Guernica made no protest against the Oviedo atrocities.

An enquiring reader who is aware that the case against Franco is based on the alleged iniquity of appealing to force against a democratically-elected Government, may be intrigued to discover how a Socialist defends the Asturian rising in 1934. He will find the answer to this question in *The Drama of Spain* by A. Ramos Oliveira, published by the National Council of Labour. Oliveira is the former editor of *El Socialista*, the central organ of the Spanish Socialist Party.

At the time of the rebellion the largest party in the Cortes was the party of the Popular Agrarians (114). The second largest party was that of the Radicals (72). Premier Lerroux invited Gil Robles to enter a coalition Government. Oliveira makes no pretence that Lerroux acted in an unconstitutional fashion or that Gil Robles had not every right both to receive and to accept an invitation to join the coalition. To create prejudice he does not describe Gil Robles' party by its proper name, the Popular Agrarians, but by a name of his own invention, "the Clericals." In the eyes of a Spanish Socialist to attend Mass is to stamp oneself as a "clerical." "When three clerical ministers," writes Oliveira, "entered the Government with the Radical Party on October 5, 1934, the Revolution broke out." And the Revolution, we are informed, "gave an epic-heroic tone to Spanish Socialism."

Armed revolution against a democratically-elected Government is "epic-heroic" when the Revolution is fermented by Moscow. On the other hand, nothing could be more wicked than to attempt to overthrow by force a Government controlled by Communists. The Right is always wrong; the Left is always right. True democracy insists not in counting noses but in counting Red noses.

In 1936 the President Alcalá Zamora dissolved the Cortes. Why? Gil Robles, still the leader of by far the largest party in the Cortes, should, by every constitutional precedent, have been invited to form a Government when all other combinations had failed. Zamora had no constitutional right to dissolve the Cortes without giving him this opportunity, but as the entry into the Government of three members of Gil Robles' party in 1934 had provoked an armed revolt, the President dared not risk another insurrection. Oliveira remarks, "Zamora to avoid another popular rising, preferred to dissolve Cortes." Nothing could be more candid. The Communists, by the threat of another revolt, terrorized the President into acting in an unconstitutional fashion. Niceto Alcalá Zamora, who brought the Popular Front into power by dissolving the Cortes, has described in the *Journal de Génève*, January 17, 1937, how the Popular Front obtained its majority.

> As to the first stage—as early as February 17, and even from the late afternoon of the 16th—the Popular Front, without awaiting the final scrutiny or the proclamation of the results of the voting, which were to be given out on February 20 by the Provincial Commissions appointed for the purpose, launched its attack by starting disorder in the streets and using violence to demand power.
>
> A Government crisis ensued, and the Civil Governors of several provinces resigned. At the urge of irresponsible

agitators, *the mob seized the balloting papers with the result that false returns were sent in from many places.*

The figures as officially given by the Spanish Government itself are:

>   Popular Front 4,356,000
>   Parties of the Right 4,570,000
>   Centre 340,000

The first statement of seats in the Cortes gave the Popular Front 256 deputies and the Right and Centre 217 deputies. The Popular Front with half a million less votes than its opponents had thirty-nine more deputies. But this majority was not sufficient to crush all opposition, and accordingly a Committee was formed to "verify the elections." Let ex-President Zamora describe the workings of this commission.

> Reinforced by such strange allies as the Basque revolutionaries, the Popular Front elected the committee entrusted with the task of verifying the elections in each constituency, a task the committee carried out in an arbitrary manner. In certain Provinces where the Opposition had been victorious, all the mandates were annulled, and candidates who were friendly to the Popular Front, *although they had been beaten*, were proclaimed deputies.
>
> Several members of minority groups were expelled from the Cortes. Nor was this done in blind party passion, but in execution of a deliberate plan conceived on a large scale. The end aimed at was two-fold—*to convert the Chamber into a packed Parliament by crushing all opposition, and to ensure the obedience of the more moderate group of the Popular Front.* As soon as the support of that group was no longer required, it became a mere puppet in the hands of the extremists.

As a result of this "verification" the Cortes took its final shape with 295 deputies of the Popular Front and 177 for the Right and Centre. The majority of 39 seats had been raised to 118.

Zamora, though he had dissolved the Cortes because of pressure from the Left, was regarded with distrust by the extremists. Señor Oliveira tells us how Zamora was removed.

> The President of the Republic was dismissed from office by Parliament in accordance with Article 81 of the Constitution. The Spanish Constitution of 1931 establishes in the aforesaid Article that the President of the Republic will consider himself dismissed if the majority of the Chamber declares that the dissolution of the previous Cortes was not justified. The Cortes of the Popular Front agreed on this indirect vote of censure and Señor Alcalá Zamora abandoned the National Palace.
>
> On the admission of Señor Oliveira his friends would have created a rising if poor Señor Zamora had not dissolved the Cortes. He tells us himself that 'it was necessary to replace the president of the Republic, who was guilty in great part for the unchaining of the Revolution in October 1934, which occurred because he gave entry to power to the Fascists.' There is probably no need to warn the reader that in this kind of literature 'Fascist' may mean anybody who wears a collar and tie. The point to be observed is that, by acting in a constitutional manner, the unfortunate President is guilty of 'unchaining a revolution.' Desirous of being 'guiltless of his country's blood' he then acts in an unconstitutional manner and is solemnly dismissed by the people under whose threats he acted. When revolt comes from the Right it must be placed on trial for it. When it comes from the Left, the Right must be placed on trial again—for 'unchaining a revolution'!

After the election was over the nominal leaders of the Popular Front were soon put in their place. "How can we accomplish a revolution without shooting?" Lenin once exclaimed. "The victory of the proletariat," he insisted, "can only be achieved by rivers of blood." "Our programme," wrote *Pravda,* September 9, 1928, "Is an all embracing and blood-soaked reality." It is certainly that—in Spain as in Russia.

On June 16 Gil Robles presented a balance sheet of "blood-soaked reality." One thousand two hundred and eighty-seven people had been injured, and 269 killed; 160 churches had been totally destroyed and 251 had been partially destroyed. Ten newspaper offices had been destroyed, and sixty-nine premises of political and other associations. These outrages were communicated in detail to the Madrid Parliament on three occasions. once by Calvo Sotelo and once by Gil Robles. These statements were not denied. They were published in the official parliamentary records and in the public Press.

The tabulated outrages include only a proportion of those which were actually committed. One example will suffice. In Madrid the Reds spread a rumour that nuns were giving poisoned sweets to the children, and a French lady who unwittingly gave some chocolate to a child was stoned to death.

Manuel Azaña's Liberal and Democratic government did nothing to stop these outrages. The police were instructed not to interfere, springing to action only to arrest citizens courageous enough to protect fellow-citizens from assault and churches from burning. The fire brigade were instructed to stand by to prevent fires spreading—from a church. To cry "Long live Spain!" in public was to invite death.

Meanwhile the deputies of the Right continued to attend the Cortes and to plead for the restoration of law and order, a very provocative thing to do it seems. "The Right," says Oliveira, "did all they could to maintain a situation of terrorism in the street." Read this sentence carefully. It is not a misprint. Robles, so Oliveira implies, was really very anxious that "the situation of terrorism" should continue because there was nothing that pleased him more than the assassination of his friends and the burning of churches. "Their method," continues Oliveira, "was to bring the Government into disrepute by presenting it as incapable of maintaining order or guaranteeing the personal security of citizens."

Of course, these outrages provoked reprisals: several times the Duchess of Atholl has drawn attention to this fact. The Duchess does not deny the epidemic of murder which provoked the Franco rising, and she does not realize that the few inevitable reprisals weaken rather than strengthen her case. A Government powerless to maintain order, and unable to prevent outrages from the Left or reprisals from the Right, has lost its moral right to rule. If the Popular Front came into power in Great Britain, and if, among other victims, the Duchess of Atholl were murdered, I hope and believe that Scotland would produce men with enough spirit to avenge her death.

The Marquis Merry del Val writes:

> The men of the Right were howled down by their masculine and feminine colleagues, with the grossest insults and the most barefaced threats. Time and again they were told that they would not leave the House alive. Pistols were brandished in their faces, both in the chamber and in the lobbies. Personal violence was incessantly attempted against them. It was enough that they should propose or attempt to defend any measure, however neutral in its character or necessary for the welfare of the State, for it to be immediately rejected. Their uninterrupted presence in Parliament and their bold and eloquent protests should always be remembered as one of the finest records of moral and physical courage. Calvo Sotelo, the bravest, the most talented, the most knowledgeable, and the most eloquent of them all, ended, by dint of perseverance and sound reasoning, in making himself heard. He at once was looked upon as a danger by the Red revolutionary leaders. They grew afraid that their adherents might, from listeners, become converts to his views on the social problem. They

determined to get him out of the way. His speedy end was announced by a female fury, Dolores Ibarruri, the self-styled *'Pasionaria'* (Passion Flower). Five nights after his last great speech in Parliament his door opened to the summons of a squad of uniformed 'Shock Police' who had left their barracks with the consent of their chiefs, and probably the connivance of the Home Secretary. Inveigled by their false representations, Señor Calvo Sotelo followed them. At three o'clock that morning his dead body was delivered to the guardians of Madrid's principal cemetery, without any dissimulation or explanation by his captors.

"You have made your last speech," screamed Pasionaria. She was right. Those who loved Spain knew that this last speech of Sotelo was the last despairing effort to save Spain by persuasion. His murder proved that there was no place for legal opposition in the Cortes, and no hope for Spain save the sword.

Let those who maintain that the revolution began when Franco rose, read *Three Pictures of the Spanish Civil War*. A Nationalist and a self-styled Democrat sum up respectively the case for Franco and the case for the Madrid Government. A Liberal who dislikes both Fascism and Communism sums up "For Spain" writing under the pseudonym of "Don Justo Medio." Here is what he says:

> The argument with which 'Democrat' seeks to prove that the insurgents had long ago planned their revolution does not greatly impress me, for the facts he gives could be quite adequately explained by the supposition that the preparations were made in order to circumvent the proletarian revolution, and the workers spoke and wrote so freely of this that no one abreast of recent Spanish history can pretend to be ignorant of it. In fact, both the Madrid and the Barcelona papers—even the respectable ones—describe the Government forces as the 'revolutionaries' and the insurgents as the 'counter-revolutionaries.' One Syndicalist paper which I occasionally buy describes itself as 'Diario de la Revolución.' This gives away

the workers' case entirely. 'Of *what* revolution,' one asks, 'is this paper the organ?' 'Of the workers' revolution,' is the reply. 'But is it not the wicked Fascists who are the revolutionaries?' . . . a convincing reply to this question would be of great interest, but it has yet to be made.

The answer asked for by "Don Justo Medio" has been provided. Cecil Gerahty, in his book *The Road to Madrid*, gives a translation of the secret document found in the Communist headquarters at La Linea. Several other copies of this document have since been discovered.

The document contains detailed plans for a Communist revolution, and lists of those who are to constitute the National Soviet, a list headed by President Largo Caballero.

The rising did not take place on the first date suggested in this document, but though postponed the plan was not abandoned. Mr. Gerahty found in Triana, a working class suburb of Seville, a circular giving July 25 as "the day arranged for our vengeance." This date was one week after the war broke out. Franco was just in time. The following is a translation of a significant extract from the confidential report.

> The signal for beginning the movement will be the bursting of five small bombs at nightfall. Immediately thereafter a pretended Fascist attack on the Club of the C.N.T. (National Confederation of Labour) will be staged, a general strike will be declared, and the soldiers implicated will rise in the barracks. The 'radios' will begin to act, the T.U.V. undertaking to seize the General Post and Telegraph Office, the Prime Minister's Office, and the Ministry of War. The district 'radios' will attack the Police Stations, and the X.Y.Z. the Police Headquarters. A special 'radio' composed solely of machine-gunners and bombers will attack the Ministry of 'Gobernación' (Interior) from the following streets: Carretas; Montera; Mayor; Correos; Paz; Alcalá; Preciados; Carmen and San Gerónimo. The radios will act with fifty cells of ten men each,

in the streets of secondary and tertiary importance, and with only two cells in the streets of first importance and avenues.

The orders are for all anti-revolutionaries to be immediately executed. The revolutionaries of the Popular Front will be called upon to second the movement and, should they refuse to do so, will be expelled from Spain.

It is easy to draw blank cheques on the future; easy to assert but impossible to prove that had Franco not risen Spain would have evolved a moderate, democratic Government. This statement has often been made, but in view of the facts summarized in this chapter, I should be interested to know what is the evidence for this hypothesis. According to the propagandists of the Left, a group of Spanish reactionaries, alarmed by the determination of the Popular Front to introduce far-reaching reforms, called upon General Franco to lead an armed revolt in order to substitute Fascism for Democracy. It is difficult to understand why reactionaries determined to oppose democracy by armed force should have failed to strike when all the odds were in their favour, and postponed the revolution until they had only a precarious chance of success. The King need never have abdicated, and in fact, had been urged to remain. He could have held Madrid from within and declared a dictatorship at the cost of perhaps a hundred lives.

The Left Wing have exploited an impatient outburst by Gil Robles in a speech he delivered October 15, 1933: "We must move towards a new state, and for that duties and sacrifices must be imposed! What matters if it means shedding blood? We need an integral power, and that is what we are seeking. In order to realize that ideal we will not detain ourselves in archaic forms. Democracy is, for us, not an end but the means to go on with the conquest of a new state. When the moment comes, either Parliament will submit, or we shall make it disappear."

Gil Robles, like everybody who knows Spain, realized

that Parliamentary democracy is unsuitable to the Spanish temperament. The theme of his speech is that he himself was seeking for some new form of democracy not unlike "organic democracy," a phrase invented, I believe, by that great Liberal, Salvador de Madariaga, whose book *Anarchy and Hierarchy* may be commended.

I have heard Gil Robles soundly abused by Spaniards of the Right for his refusal to entertain the idea of dictatorship; they saw even more clearly than he the necessity to forestall a Red revolution, but their warnings were disregarded. Gil Robles should be judged not by one speech but by his career as a whole. In 1935, the local Conservatives, alarmed by the Communist rising in 1934, once again begged Gil Robles to seize power by a *coup d'état*. He refused, and in a public speech he declared, "We are asked to carry out a *coup d'état*. We will not. I will not forget my duty, nor will the Army forget its duty to proper authority. A *coup d'état* is for a defeated minority" (he was referring to the Communist rising, just crushed), "and not for a party that has the nation with it. When the time comes, we will take power from the hands of the nation. In the words of Cisneros: 'These are our powers, these are our army—the people of Spain.'"

The story of Spain from 1931 to 1936 may be summed up in a few words. The King abdicated when he could have seized power, and the Conservatives refused to attempt a *coup d'état*, for both the King and the Conservatives were determined to give democracy a chance. Democracy has perished in Spain because the Communists were determined that democracy should fail, and that the Popular Front should be nothing more than a "transitional form" leading to a Red dictatorship.

It is true that the King asked General Primo de Rivera to establish a dictatorship as the only possible solution in a time of tragic disorder, in the course of which the Cardinal Archbishop of Saragossa had been murdered. During the eight years of the dictatorship Spain made more material progress than during any similar period of the last two centuries.

Finally, here are two quotations for those who still persist in the illusion that Red Spain believes in democracy. The first is from Señor Oliveira, selected by the National Council of Labour to state the Red case. He tells us that within a year of the institution of the Republic events had proved *"the almost utter impossibility of acclaiming Western democracy on Spanish soil."*

My second quotation is from a speech delivered by that great democrat, Largo Caballero, in 1934. *"What is the use of liberty? Is not the State by definition an absolute power? Certainly we Socialists and true Republicans are not going to be foolish enough to grant liberty if, at the first opportunity, it undermines the foundations of Government."*[1]

And to those innocent people who still attempt to assess the strength of Communism in Spain by the number of Communists in the Cortes, let me reply in the words of Dimitrov:

"Only the Communist Party is at bottom the initiator, the organizer, and the driving force of the United Front."

---

[1] Quoted by Peers, p. 158.

5 FOREIGN INTERVENTION

"Any moral condemnation of civil war is intolerable from a Marxist standpoint."
                                                            Lenin.

I HAVE shown that Russian intervention antedated German and Italian intervention by many years, that Franco rose only just in time to anticipate a Communist revolution, and that the strength of Communism in Spain cannot be measured by the number of self-declared Communists, because Communism works through a Communist penumbra of sympathetic Socialists. In spite of violent differences between Communists and Anarchists, both Communists and Anarchists agree on the necessity of eliminating the middle class and on the value of terrorism as a weapon in the class struggle.

I can understand the position of an extreme pacifist who condemns without reservation all use of physical force, but those who evade the claim that Franco was justified in rising, by repeating with parrot-like insistence *that* he rose, are either exceptionally foolish or exceptionally uncandid. They forget that Great Britain, the United States, France, the Italy which Garibaldi united, the Greece which cast off the Turks, to say nothing of Russia, all owe their modern forms to revolutionary movements. It is those who are loudest in the praise of the Russian revolution who affect to be most shocked by Franco.

"To turn to the responsibility for intervention," writes Sir Francis Lindley, formerly our Ambassador in Madrid, "there is even less doubt on which side the fault lies than there is in the atrocities question. The policy of Moscow, openly proclaimed and not, therefore, in dispute, is to prepare and organize revolution abroad by means of liberally-financed agents, and, if it [revolution] should break out, support it with men and materiel."

Since both Governments in Spain conceal the number of their own volunteers and exaggerate the number of volunteers fighting for the enemy, it is impossible to estimate exactly, and futile to guess, which view is correct. Certain facts at any rate can be ascertained.

No Germans are fighting with the infantry of the Nationalist army because Hitler dreaded the possibility that German and French volunteers might oppose each other in the trenches. Air duels between individual Germans and French have a less dangerous effect on the two countries. The main service of the Germans has been to provide technical advisers behind the lines. They have been particularly useful in the anti-aircraft department.

That Italy has sent regular officers is certain, but it is improbable that units of the regular Italian army are serving in Spain.

I spent five hours in Spain with a volunteer who was half English and half Spanish, more English in many ways than Spanish. His work had brought him into close contact with the Italians, and he told me that the Italians he met were volunteers from the upper and middle classes, for the most part inexperienced amateur soldiers with more gallantry than skill. When they landed in Spain there had been a call for volunteers to drive lorries. Every Italian believes that he is a born driver by divine right, and among the casualties due to this conviction were a number of damaged lorries and two lamp posts removed from the pavements in Seville.

The proposal to withdraw volunteers appears, at the time

of writing, to raise some difficulties. Most of the volunteers who were fighting for the Valencia Government surrendered the passports they had, and are now Spanish citizens with Spanish passports. The International Column includes many men who cannot return to their own countries, anti-Fascist Italians and anti-Nazi Germans. Most of them would be unwelcome in any country save in Russia or France, and many of them might have some difficulty in obtaining permission to remain in France. The withdrawal of volunteers would therefore operate greatly to the advantage of the Valencia Government.

The British public are less interested in the question of numbers than in the alleged motives for the German and Italian intervention. Nobody who has ever seen, lived in, or travelled through a country where Communism was in complete or in partial control can doubt that the main motive of the German and Italian intervention is to prevent the establishment of a Soviet state on the shores of the Mediterranean.

Mr. Anthony Eden has recently declared that Great Britain would not tolerate any attack upon the territorial integrity of Spain, and he has implied that we should be prepared to go to war to prevent Italy gaining a foothold on Spanish soil. Is it therefore so surprising that Italy and Germany are determined to prevent Spain becoming a Soviet colony? If Communism wins in Spain, Russia will have captured a key position commanding the passage between the Atlantic and the Mediterranean, and separated only by the Straits of Gibraltar from North Africa, the Africa Russia is determined to infect with the Communist virus. Nor will the Pyrenees, crossed by thousands of French volunteers who have poured into Spain to fight for Communism, prove an effective barrier against infection from a Communist Spain.

Our interest in maintaining the territorial integrity of Spain is certainly no greater than Mussolini's interest in maintaining the spiritual integrity of the Iberian Peninsula. Mussolini and Franco have explicitly denied that there were territorial bargains in return for Italian assistance, and Franco certainly has given proof that, whatever the cost, he is prepared to maintain a united Spain. He refused to make terms with the Basques extremists, but for whose opposition the war would have ended long ago in a victory for the Nationalists. A well-known Nationalist slogan is "Better a Red Spain than a divided Spain."

The Valencia Government, on the other hand, attempted to secure British and French support by offering these powers territorial concessions in Spanish Morocco.

Sir Francis Lindley, formerly Ambassador in Madrid, who believes that we have everything to gain from a victory for Franco, writes as follows:

> When you are warned against a great danger or advised to take some serious action, you naturally examine the credentials of those who warn or advise you. If we so treat those who are loudest in declaring that a victory for General Franco will constitute a dangerous threat to the British Empire, we shall find that these are the very people who, on all other occasions, have paraded their dislike of and contempt for that Empire. So we naturally conclude that the victory they fear will be the best outcome as regards our Imperial interests. This conclusion is correct as an impartial examination of the position makes manifest.
>
> I suppose no one doubts now that a Red victory in Spain means a Soviet State directed from Moscow. Catalonia is already such a State, and the rest of Spain will become one if General Franco is beaten. The first result of this would be the total destruction of British property and the cessation of all British enterprise in Spain. There are a number of people in this country who would regard such a development with complacency; but that does not alter the fact that it is our resources abroad, accumulated through the energy and enterprise of generations of British subjects, which enable our population to enjoy a standard of living higher than in any

country of Europe or Asia. And British assets in Spain form no negligible part of those resources.

The notion that a Soviet victory would conjure the danger of excessive German or Italian influence in the Western Mediterranean is a delusion. Should a Soviet State be set up in Spain, the danger of Germany entrenching herself in some Spanish possession in order to counteract Bolshevik activities becomes a very real one. General Franco, on the other hand, is fighting for Spanish unity and it is highly improbable that he would consent in the hour of victory to cede any part of the Spanish dominions. Italy is a little off the map as a bogey after the recent Anglo-Italian exchange of Notes; but, while the same argument applies to her as to Germany, her geographical position already makes the friendliest relations with Great Britain an imperious necessity for both countries.

Even if Franco were ready to surrender Spanish territory, he could not make Mussolini a present of Gibraltar without first capturing Gibraltar from Great Britain. We shall lose Gibraltar when we are defeated in a war with Great Britain on one side and Spain and Italy on the other, but if we are defeated in such a war, the loss of Gibraltar will be a relatively unimportant detail compared with the loss of our imperial power. Gibraltar has no intrinsic value save as an imperial fortress. If we cease to be an imperial power we shall have no more interest in the Mediterranean than Norway has to-day. If we are defeated in war we shall lose Gibraltar; if we are not defeated in war we shall hold Gibraltar. The Gibraltar complex is therefore irrational, and our attention should be concentrated not on this isolated rock but on the general problem of rearmament. There would be no need to dread the possibility of war with Italy if only our pacifist warmongers would not wreck every attempt to renew the traditional friendship between Italy and England.

Fascism is not for export. Italy, unlike Russia, is not subsidizing agents of revolution in England. Every

Communist in Great Britain or in the United States, as in Spain in the past, is the agent of a foreign power publicly proclaiming as its policy the corruption of the armed forces as a preparation for civil war. The interests of peace are best served, not by friendship with the agents of the Third International but by an attitude of watchful hostility to those who preach peace in the League of Nations while preparing, in their own words, "to transform every imperial war into a civil war."

6 RED PROPAGANDA

THE SPANISH REDS have proved themselves apt disciples of those great masters of propaganda, the Russian Communists. If the war could have been won on the air and in the Press, the Reds would long ago have been victorious in spite of their defeat in the air and on the field.

There are two main branches of Red propaganda and it is important to distinguish between them. First there is political exaggeration, the suppression of inconvenient facts, and the most favourable interpretation of provable facts. This form of propaganda is normal in wartime, and has been used by both the Nationalists and the Reds. Secondly there is the deliberate circulation of lies. Characteristic examples of the first form of propaganda are the slogans that the Spanish War is a war between democracy and Fascism, and the exploitation of the accidental and misleading associations of words such as "Right Wing" and "Left Wing." The Valencia Government have been very successful in arousing the sympathy of working classes throughout the world for their cause, and their success is due to the fact that "Right Wing" suggests a united front of capitalists and reactionaries, whereas "Left Wing" still suggests a united front not of politicians on the make, but of idealists with a sincere passion for social justice.

A point often made by Left-Wing propagandists is that Franco must be fighting for Capitalism since he has been financed by capitalists. He has been financed partly by the rich and partly by the poor. The Valencia Government has the backing of one of the richest men in France, M. Léon Blum, and of many of the leading newspapers in this country neither owned nor controlled by the proletariat.

Only the ill-informed genuinely believe that the Nationalists are less concerned than the Popular Front to redress the grievances of the poor. Carlists and Phalangists broadly agree on a social policy, sternly anti-capitalist, for the Nationalists are determined that in the new Spain the producer shall not be at the mercy of the banker. The policy of the new Spain does not only exist on paper as an utopian dream. It has already been practiced and enforced in territory for many months under Nationalist control.

The correspondent of *The Tablet* writes on May 15, 1937:

> All contracts of work in existence on July 18, 1936 have been declared valid and renewed. In order to guarantee the rights of the workmen there have been established in each province a certain number of Inspectors of Work, who are State functionaries, visiting factories and workshops to see whether the conditions of work are carried out, and supervising masters and employees in order to verify faults, which are immediately corrected and punished with heavy fines.
>
> Before a workman may be dismissed, an authorization from the "Provincial Delegate of Work" is necessary. This official is a kind of "Prefect of Work" attached to each province and examining labour problems as they arise. When the Delegate of Work receives an application from an employer to dismiss a workman, master and man are summoned to give evidence so that the Delegate may adjudicate the case. If the dismissal is granted, there may still be an appeal to a "Tribunal of Work,"

consisting of three employers, three workers and an officially appointed presiding magistrate. If an employer dismisses a worker without permission, or after having been refused permission by the Delegate of Work, he is obliged to readmit him and to pay him the arrears of wages from the date of his dismissal to his readmission. . . .

The facts enumerated in this article, and the declarations of policy published by the Carlists and the Phalangists, refute the "rich v. poor" propaganda.

The Reds do not confine themselves to distortion of the truth but are completely reckless in their circulation of lies. Douglas Jerrold was at Toledo on the day when heavy fighting in Toledo was reported on the wireless. He did not hear a shot fired. A few days later I visited Toledo and asked for details of the recent battle.

"Battle in Toledo?" said my companion in a puzzled tone. "Collect yourself, my dear Lunn. Look at the Tagus gorge."

We were standing at a window of the Alcázar. I looked across at the Red lines and realised that a minor campaign would be necessary before the Reds could again penetrate into Toledo.

More than once in this war Red militiamen have strolled unconcernedly into villages captured by the Reds—on paper—only to be arrested by Nationalists who had held the village continuously since they had first captured it.

La Métropole of Belgium quotes a list compiled in Salamanca of the Government's successes gained on paper up to April 19, 1937. The total of these claims is impressive, for the Reds have won one and a half million square kilometres, three times the total surface area of Spain, and killed and wounded two and a half million of their enemies, captured 345,000 prisoners; have taken 415,000 cannons, 775,000 machine-guns; and have shot down 56,770 aeroplanes. They have captured Huesca twenty-six times, Toledo eleven, Oviedo twenty-two times.

Peadar O'Donnel, an Irishman who sympathises with the Reds, and whose book *Salud!* is a vivid and moving description of Catalonia during the war, makes some entertaining comments on the Barcelona publicity service. "The service," he writes, "just shrieked with victories, proclamations, denunciations, and all that wide swiping which makes war news so ridiculous. The Anarchists alone ran a really readable paper, and that was mainly because they did tell stories of real happenings, and reflected workaday life in reports from the syndicates, but even they captured the same village far too often."

The most disagreeable form of Red propaganda is the deliberate policy of using women and children as a shield for their retreating troops.

Señor Rugeroni told me in Seville that on entering a village captured from the Reds he had been met by a group of thirty-five women who held their hands in front of their breasts and exclaimed, "For the love of God, don't cut them off." The retreating Reds urged them to fly, and assured them that they would be cut to pieces by the Fascists.

The motives of this lie are clear. The retreating Reds hoped to enjoy an ignominious protection if only they could persuade a confused and terrified mob of women and children to retreat with them. After retreating from Málaga the Reds accused Nationalists of shelling the road used by the fleeing refugees.

"I myself happened to be there," writes Captain Bolín, "and I can swear that no attack took place, that on the contrary the troops helped the refugees in every way, going to the extent of giving them food and remaining without any themselves for at least a whole day. Incidentally, there would have been no refugees had not the Reds terrorized the inhabitants of Málaga and forced them to leave their homes, thereby inflicting upon them untold misery and suffering."

The Nationalists have often foregone military advantages

rather than inflict heavy losses on the civilian population, for it must not be forgotten that to the Nationalists the civilians behind the Red lines are not "the enemy" but fellow Spaniards to be rescued from oppression. Many civilians have undoubtedly been killed in Madrid, but Franco warned the Reds of the bombardment and asked them to evacuate non-combatants.

The case for Franco on this issue was admirably stated by a group of Conservative M.P.'s in the following letter to *The Times:*

> Sir,—In your issue of December 5 you print from an address in the Haymarket an appeal to the Government to refuse to recognize General Franco. This is signed by distinguished individuals of various political parties who have found a common platform in their wish to protest publicly against the wickedness of the Spanish National leader in permitting "the bombardment of Madrid or the attempt to starve it into surrender."
>
> It is worth while asking the signatories to this letter to draw upon their military experience and to tell us exactly what tactics they would pursue if they were in General Franco's place. Can they suggest more humane methods of subduing this large town, which the Communist and Anarchist rump of the "constitutionally elected Spanish Government" has turned into a fortress by constructing barricades and trenches and by arming the dregs of the population, and is defending by an international brigade, armed in breach of the Non-Intervention Agreement and manned in defiance of its spirit? Is it suggested that the National artillery and aircraft should remain inactive for fear of killing civilians, and that General Franco should send his men into the narrow streets to be shot down by snipers sitting in safety in the houses on either side? All we know of General Franco is that he is a gallant soldier. He has been goaded into action not by personal ambition but by witnessing the increasing outrages in Spain under a Government that in its subservience to the Left refused to govern. His rising only forestalled by a few days the projected Red revolution.
>
> Surely it is charitable to allow that, since in his opinion to

save Spain he must occupy Madrid, he use only shell and bomb as dire necessities in the knowledge that his own countrymen, and even his own sympathizers, must suffer, as well as the international gangsters his opponents have called in to fight their battle. He has done what he can to save non-combatants by setting aside a large part of the capital which he has undertaken to refrain from bombing.

> We are, etc.,
> ALFRED KNOX, NAIRNE SANDEMAN,
> COOPER RAWSON, ALAN GRAHAM,
> E. A. TAYLOR, VICTOR RAIKES.

House of Commons, *Dec. 8.*

7 THE IRRESPONSIBILITY OF THE LEFT

THE FINE ART of dialectics is disappearing from the modern world. Men no longer debate; they denounce. It is, of course, easy to understand why Communists should prefer denunciation to debate, for debate is only possible between opponents who appeal to a standard of ethics both accept. The Communist denies the existence of objective morality. Those actions are good which help, and those are bad which injure, the cause of Communism. Whatever the Reds do is right, and whatever the Rights do is wrong. This doctrine has its value as a rule of faith, but it is of little use as a basis of discussion between Communists and their opponents. The application of this doctrine to propaganda may be illustrated by a few striking examples.

Nothing could be more dishonest than to pose, as Communists are instructed to pose, as the friends of democracy in Great Britain and in Spain. Communists, by definition, have contrived to replace democracy by a dictatorship of the proletariat. Nothing is more fatuous than the contrast between the uncritical praise lavished by Communists on the Russian dictatorship, and the no less uncritical abuse of Hitler and Mussolini.

The Left Wing who are so indignant with Franco for rising against a democratically-elected Government were equally indignant in 1934 when a democratically-elected Republican Government put down by force a Moscow-inspired rising of the Asturian miners. "The very publicists," writes Arthur Bryant, "who are now demanding British intervention and a world war in order to assert the inalienable rights of legally-constituted government were only two years before justifying rebellion against an equally legally-constituted government. It is fortunate for these illogical warmongers that the memory of the British public is so short."

Our Left Wing never tire of denouncing the persecution of intellectuals in Italy and Germany, but with a few and honourable exceptions have remained silent on the infinitely more tragic suppression of intellectual life in Russia.

It is logical to deplore foreign intervention in the Spanish civil war. It is irrational to protest indignantly because the Italians and the Germans are helping Franco while continuing to applaud the intervention of Russia and France.

I can understand all those who denounce bombing from the air as inhuman, but I cannot understand the position of men who are indignant when Guernica is bombed and who raise no protest against the bombing of Saragossa, Talavera, Seville, Avila or Granada.

I have just read *Death in the Morning* by Helen Nicholson, a beautiful and moving account of life in Granada during the first two months of the war. Granada was never in the hands of the Reds, nor did the Reds make any serious attempt to capture it. On the outbreak of the war the White garrison seized Granada and have held it continuously up to this day. In the early days of the war they had no anti-aircraft guns and their few antiquated aeroplanes were of little use against modern bombing planes. Granada was constantly bombed, but no attempt was made to attack it from the ground. The bombing was not designed as a preparation for military attack.

I have just read a review of this book in the *Manchester Guardian*. "Unhappily," writes the reviewer, "all the evidence of the war goes to show that it is impossible in bombardment of towns used as military centres to avoid hitting civilians. There is no proof that the killing of civilians was of deliberate intention."

Probably not. But the *Manchester Guardian* took a very different tone when Guernica, unlike Granada, on the fringe of a battle zone, and unlike Granada, a centre for the making of munitions, was alleged rightly or wrongly to have been bombed by German aeroplanes.

Even more disedifying than the inconsequence is the irresponsibility of Left-Wing propaganda. The reckless way in which charges are made is only equalled by the insouciance with which these charges are abandoned—they are, of course, never formally withdrawn. Mud-slinging takes the place of substantiated attacks. I should define mud-slinging as abuse unsupported by evidence, and mud-slinging is an accepted method of Red propaganda.

My first examples are taken from a book, *Behind the Spanish Barricades*, by John Langdon-Davies. I liked many things about this book. Mr. Langdon-Davies knows and loves Spain, and he writes with passionate enthusiasm of its people. I prefer a fanatic of the Left to superior persons who dismiss the Spanish tragedy by saying, "One side or the other, it makes no difference."

"I think," writes Mr. Langdon-Davies, "one side right and the other criminally wrong," and because I agree with him on this point I have read his book with a certain sympathy, radically though I disagree with his views on the origin of the war. But the value of his book as an historical record of these events is ruined by his irresponsibility. He tells us that a Catholic paper, the *A.B.C. of Córdoba*, published a statement that the Bishop of Pamplona has just granted "a hundred days' plenary indulgence to anyone killing a Marxist."

When Mr. Langdon-Davies was informed that a plenary indulgence by definition cannot be limited to any period time, and that the phrase "a hundred days' plenary indulgence" is therefore nonsense, he made some contemptuous remark about "quibbles," but the point at issue is not the distinction between one kind of indulgence and another, but the accuracy of a writer who, while professing to quote from a Catholic paper, attributes to that paper an elementary mistake no Catholic editor or contributor could have been guilty of making. Since the alleged extract cannot be genuine, we need not waste time proving that Catholic bishops do not grant indulgences for killing Marxists. Mr. Langdon-Davies is an honest man, and he has clearly been the victim of a fraud.

On page 284 of his book I found this statement: "Yet Toledo was taken. Machine has triumphed over man. The men in my photograph were burned to death or shot against a wall."

I wrote to Mr. Langdon-Davies and asked if there was any evidence for this statement. He replied, "The evidence for what happened when the rebels took Toledo can be found in news agency reports and in various reputable newspapers. . . ." He gave no references and he added, "No doubt the Press Attaché at the Spanish Embassy can assist you with details."

I wrote to the Spanish Embassy and asked them if there was any evidence in support of Mr. Langdon-Davies' charges; they replied as follows:

EMBAJADA DE ESPAÑA,
24, BELGRAVE SQUARE,
LONDON, S.W. 1.

Dear Sir,

The Spanish Ambassador has asked me to reply to your letter of July 1st, and to say that he has no knowledge of the statement in question. Mr. Langdon-Davies has not communicated with us on the subject, and we are not in a position to say what was the source of his information.

I am sorry that we cannot help you in this matter.

Yours faithfully,
STANLEY RICHARDSON.

Mr. Langdon-Davies was in Toledo during the siege of the Alcázar and his imaginative gifts have enabled him in his book, to reconstruct the life of the garrison which he did not share. He refers to the "implicated priests who fled to the Alcázar." One need not be well informed to know that before the mines were exploded the Reds granted a request to send a priest into the garrison to baptize babies born during the siege, hear confessions and administer the sacraments to men who had been without a priest since the siege began. Most of those who have visited Spain know that the priest in question has been severely criticized because he remained within the Alcázar only for a few hours. The "implicated priests" to whom Mr. Langdon-Davies refers, existed only in his imagination. In the following passage Mr. Langdon-Davies draws a picture of life within the Alcázar.

> If only someone could write their history; how as the days of futile agony pass some have grown cruel and others religious; some have grown beards, and others have kept themselves as clean shaven and dapper as if there was an alternative to lingering death; the stealthy hunting of women; the mothers watching their children; wondering if to-morrow there will still be a thin drop of nourishment to be squeezed from their starved breasts; the children still thinking of new games, playing Fascists versus Reds, no doubt. Some souls are

growing daily more noble beneath the strain, others are cracked and go squeaking, like bats, to hell. . . .

What on earth do they not in their feverish state confess to the priests? And some are promising themselves a life of purity if they ever get out, others a visit to the nearest brothel.

As this passage may leave an unpleasant after-taste, I will quote a statement made to Major McNeill-Ross by a man who had fought throughout the siege.

They achieved an exaltation. They came to see themselves defenders of faith, under divine protection. There was no priest with them. There were no services, except those at the burials in the riding-school. Thus, and because they were so often solitary, the faith of each individual grew. Some came to feel themselves inspired. One recalled his feelings during those days.

"We are few, they are many. But numbers are not all. We believe, we have faith. They do not believe; they would destroy faith. They think; that is in the brain. We pray; that is in the heart. I myself, sometimes I cry. But I am not afraid. If I die, I die. But that is only, myself. What I believe, cannot die.

"As I take my aim, I pray; as I throw a bomb, I pray.

"We are filthy. We have not washed. Our clothes stench. We have insects. All that is around us is reeking and disgusting. We live in filth. But we live half, away beyond it. We do not swear. We do not blaspheme. We do not allow ourselves carnal thoughts. Those who have wives within the Alcázar do not take them.

"The Reds think. Thinking is nothing. Presently they will give way. We believe. That endures forever."

8 A BRITISH VISITOR IN MADRID

E<small>VEN THOSE</small> who differ from the Duchess of Atholl on the Spanish issue respect her integrity, and realise that in defending what she believes to be true she has alienated many friends. Mr. R. G. Dawson, for instance, resigned from the Chairmanship of the Blackford Unionist Association and from the Unionist Executive Council of the Duchess's constituency. In the course of his address at a special meeting of the Executive Council held in the Conservative Club, Perth, on June 2, 1937, he said:

> Yet, Ladies and Gentlemen, the Member for this Conservative constituency, dedicated to these principles, in her recent visit to Spain metaphorically certainly, and literally probably, took the hand of friendship of Communists and even of Anarchists in Madrid and Valencia. . . . We are asked to sympathize with men who, since the outbreak of war, have put to death 15,000 priests: who have soaked suspected Nationalist sympathizers with petrol and burnt them alive: who have shot prisoners, not so as to kill, but so as to be able to bury them helpless, alive: who have made the wholesale execution of hostages a new feature in the already sufficiently ghastly

horrors of modern war; who in the towns under their control have organized murder-gangs, the members of which acting as judges one moment, and executioners the next, have cut off hundreds, whose only fault was to hope for better times. And yet against this our Member is satisfied to assure us that the prisoners she interrogated expressed themselves as contented with their treatment—as though men in the hands of such foes could be expected to do anything else!

I first met the Duchess of Atholl a few years ago when she and I attended a committee meeting founded to counteract the subversive efforts of her present allies. In those days the Duchess was much impressed by the Communist peril. None of us could have foreseen that on June 24, 1937, she would take the chair at a meeting on "Spain and Culture," in the Albert Hall; the meeting, at which Left-Wing extremists spoke, advertised among its attractions the promise of a message broadcast direct from Moscow.

I suspect that the Duchess's change of front is due not to a change of attitude towards Communism but to her dread of Nazi Germany. She regards Germany as a greater danger than Russia, and has apparently been much influenced by a book, *The Nazi Conspiracy in Spain*, already analysed in these pages.

The Duchess spent nine days in Red Spain, and was conducted round Madrid. She would seem to have been less observant than the correspondent of the *Manchester Guardian*, who sympathizes, as the Duchess does, with the Valencia Government, but who is less uncritical in his admiration for that Government. He tells us that the official records of those massacred in Madrid reached the appalling total of 35,000. "The records still exist," he writes, insisting that "the number of persons executed in Madrid alone can hardly be much less than 40,000." He goes on:

The great walls in front of which the victims in the

Chamartin de la Rosa were lined up and shot, can still be seen. They are scarred and pock-marked with bullet holes. These walls have a whitish surface with red stone or brick beneath, so that the marks are very conspicuous—there are long streaks, four or five feet up, on an average, where the white surface has been shot away altogether. There is no sight in all Spain more terrible than these walls and the great open space in front of them, where the dead lie side by side, with the earth heaped over them, in trenches of such size that the mind shrinks from trying to conjecture how many there may be.

A correspondent for *The Times* wrote in an uncensored despatch (September 26, 1936), "Daily executions—on one day there were eighty—continue in Madrid. . . . The ghastly array in the morgue has been made more horrible by the bodies of murdered women. One was the Marquesa de Silvela, wife of the Marqués, who with his younger brother was taken from his house and shot some time ago. . . . The other, Señora de Aldama, was shot because she would not reveal where her husband and son were hiding. . . . It is still sufficient to be a nobleman or a priest to be condemned to death." A Spanish nobleman, of course, for the Duchess of Atholl was in no danger.

The Times in its despatch of October 6, 1936, expressed sympathy with the citizens who "have hungered spiritually for nine long weeks. Anti-Christ has been given a long waited opportunity." The Duchess was more fortunate. She attended a Protestant chapel and told England about it.

If St. Paul's were wrecked and Westminster Abbey closed, and every honourable Anglican clergyman in hiding, what should we think of a Spanish Duchess who on her return to Spain informed her friends that she had been able to attend Mass in Red London?

In Madrid the Duchess of Atholl met the Communist Minister of Education. He assured her that the Government was anxious to reopen the churches. I hope the Duchess has not read the rude and tactless remarks on religious propaganda published for visitors in *Solidaridad Obrera*,[1] the organ of the Regional Confederation of Labour in Catalonia, quoted elsewhere in this book.

The Duchess of Atholl has much to say of Father Locardio Lobo, whom she describes as Acting-Vicar of San Gines in Madrid. *Acting*-Vicar, a pleasant sinecure to "act" as Vicar of a church that is closed. The Dean of Canterbury described this cleric as Vicar-General of Madrid. There has never been a Vicar-General of Madrid.

Nor is Father Lobo an "acting-vicar." In the course of a lecture tour he was twice challenged—in Paris and in Brussels—to produce documents to prove that he was a priest in good standing. When he failed to do so, he was excluded from the Altar. The inaccuracies of the Duchess and the Dean may not seem important, but they are some indication of the value to be placed on their "impressions." Father Lobo, at a time when every decent priest was either dead or in hiding, drove through Madrid in a car flying the Red banner. He is an agent of the Red Government.

"Father Lobo," writes the Duchess, "frankly admitted that the Catholic Church had not been blameless." No doubt Caballero admitted with equal frankness that Franco had not been blameless in the events of last July.

The Duchess was much impressed by the Minister of Justice, José García Oliver, an Anarchist; from him she extracted another "frank admission." It seems that among the extremists of the Left there have been "a good many irregular unions."

I wonder if the Minister of Justice was present at a meeting at Saragossa of the C.N.T. held just before the war, whose proceedings are described by Mr. Langdon-Davies, an ardent supporter of the Red cause, in *Behind the Spanish Barricades:*

> They passed a resolution that if anyone, male or female,

[1] January 28, 1937.

chanced to rouse the sexual feelings of another, it amounted to a gross and palpable interference with the freedom and happiness of that other, unless the guilty person was prepared to relieve the feelings he or she had produced. They therefore carried with acclamation the proposition that such persons, if they refused to alleviate the suffering they had imposed on another by rousing sexual feeling, must be exiled from the town or village where they resided for a period long enough for all fires to be quenched.

The Minister of Justice escorted the Duchess to the model prison where "political prisoners" are confined, that is to say, prisoners who, like the Duchess are of noble birth, or who, like the present writer wear a collar and sometimes a tie. The Duchess was relieved to discover that the sentences run from one year to thirty years, and that a year is remitted for twelve months of good conduct, so if all goes well, people who have been convicted for being born, like the Duchess, into the aristocracy, or for wearing collars and ties, may be released in 1952.

I wonder if the Minister of Justice quoted to the Duchess two recent remarks of his at a public meeting. "The Courts of Justice are not to be merely popular but primitive tribunals. . . . Man comes not from God but from the beasts; that is why his reactions are those of a beast," except, of course, when he is talking to a British Duchess. Spanish Duchesses have to resign themselves to the more normal reactions.

The Minister of Justice is an authority on prison life, for he is familiar as an inmate with Spanish prisons in which he has served long terms for common crimes.

The Duchess, of course, admits that atrocities have taken place in Red Spain, and advances the usual excuse that the Government were powerless to prevent these owing to the fact that Franco's insurrection robbed them not only of the Army but of most of the police. The excuse is unconvincing, for the Red forces contain thousands of soldiers and

Civil Guards who could as easily have been coerced into restoring order as into fighting on the side of the Reds. Moreover, the Duchess forgets that the Red Terror which provoked this revolt occurred while the army and police were still at the disposal of the Popular Front Government, and that this Government took no steps to prevent the massacre of political opponents, the burning of churches and the destruction of newspaper offices.

The Duchess sees no inconsistency in asking our sympathy for a Government which she represents as democratic, orderly and in control of the situation, and expecting us to acquit the Government of complicity in a persecution as terrible as Diocletian's, on the ground that the Government could not maintain order. The recent internecine street battles at Barcelona reinforce the second and refute the first of these mutually contradictory pleas.

The Duchess, who is impressed by the small number of Communists in the Government, would be less impressed if she had studied the new tactics of Moscow, the advance by "partial slogans." Here is a quotation from *La Vanguardia* of Barcelona. "The trick by which they [the Communist Party] do not appear in the Government with any greater preponderance than before is too naïve to deceive anyone." Sanguine *Vanguardia*. The trick has succeeded all too well—in England.

The Times correspondent, who spent rather longer than nine days in Madrid, was not so easily hoodwinked. "Madrid," he wrote in an uncensored despatch on November 21, 1936, "is inundated with Moscow posters to which the Spanish captions have been set, plastering the walls, while the cinemas give endless series of Communist films."

In an article in *The Empire Review* the Duchess stated that she had been supplied with a list of pastors and evangelists executed by the Insurgents. I challenged her to produce this list. I pointed out that the Burgos Government publishes the names of the victims and dates and places of the crimes, and I asked the Duchess to be equally precise and to give the names of the alleged victims and to prove that they were executed *qua* pastors and not *qua* Reds. On the second point she remained silent, and on the first she quotes a statement of a Mr. King that "he is not at liberty to give the names and addresses of the sufferers."

Their address is presumably Heaven, and it is difficult to see why the Duchess should be reluctant to publish names of these pastors unless her allies suspect that the pastors have not been executed. *Habeas corpus* is an accepted principle of British law, *Ne habeas nomen* of Red propaganda.

In the course of a conversation in Spain I was assured that a pastor alleged to have been executed was alive and flourishing, but as I have not obtained evidence to support this assertion, I do not expect the Duchess to attach any truth to it. My standards of evidence are more exacting than hers. Meanwhile *quod gratis asseritur, gratis negatur*. I deny that any pastors have been executed, and I suggest that the Duchess has brought unsubstantial charges of murder.

I also asked the Duchess to reply to this question. No great Spanish leader in opposition to the Popular Front in Feburary 1935 has seceded to the Government, but many of the most respected leaders of Spanish Liberalism and Radicalism have deserted the Popular Front.

It was irrelevant to reply, as the Duchess did, by a catena of names of politicians who have supported the Government from its foundation, and it was ungenerous to reply by suggesting that scholars of European reputation, such as Dr. Gregorio Marañón and Miguel de Unamuno, had been influenced by the desire to join the winning side. Men are not necessarily base because their views today resemble those once professed by the Duchess.

The Duchess attempted to discredit Dr. Marañón because

he signed an anti-Franco declaration of the intellectuals on July 30. According to the Madrid correspondent of *The Times*, writing in the issue for July 2, 1937, most of those who signed the Manifesto of the intellectuals to which the Duchess of Atholl attaches so much importance, "have since left the Republic; several have sons serving with the Nationalists. Yet the pamphlet circulates."

I do not blame men who resort to a somewhat unheroic subterfuge to escape from the attack of terrorists. By attempting to discredit Dr. Marañón the Duchess of Atholl has only succeeded in discrediting the Government she defends. A Government that forces professors to sign declarations when their subsequent conduct proves they do not believe in these declarations, is a Government no honest intellectual in other countries can support. These signatures are worth no more than "voluntary" confessions, a routine fixture in the state trials in Soviet Russia.

It is clear that the Duchess of Atholl has never studied the Communist technique for impressing visiting delegations. As explained in *I was a Soviet Worker*, Andrew Smith spent some years in Russia, and returned to expose one of the most brutal rackets that the world has ever seen. In his book he explains how hospitals are rigged for the benefit of simple visitors, and then gives us a picture of a hospital where a disillusioned American Communist died.

> The next day my wife and I went to the hospital to visit Knotek. He was lying on a bed of boards without springs, in a cold, dark, narrow corridor. His lips and tongue were black, and he was burning with fever. He lay uncared for in the midst of his own excrement. When I saw the terrible condition the boy was in, I immediately demanded to see the chief doctor, to whom I complained bitterly. He explained that the boy was going to die anyway, so there was no use bothering with him.

It was a Russian who devised the technique of camouflage bearing his name in the phrase "Potemkin villages." The Empress Catherine of Russia liked to feel that her people loved her, and when she journeyed through the Crimea she demanded evidence of this love. The story is that Potemkin, with the co-operation of the Director of the National Theatre, arranged for model villages to be built along the route of her journey, and actors to impersonate cheering and enthusiastic villagers. The Communists in Russia and in Spain have mastered the Potemkin technique and applied it with success to model prisons and model hospitals. It seems to have been as successful with Katharine, Duchess of Atholl, as with Catherine, Empress of Russia.

9 "NOTHING LEFT TO PERSECUTE"

> *"The things I want my Church to stand for lie behind what Russia has done."*
>
> The Dean of Canterbury.
>
> *"The attitude of some of our highly-placed divines is stupefying, and to me personally, as a life-long member of the Church of England, revolting."*
>
> Sir Francis Lindley.

THE *Manchester Guardian* in its issue of June 24, 1937, published an illuminating article by a special correspondent who had just returned from Spain.

> The attack on religion has been more radical in loyalist Spain than anywhere else in the world, including even Mexico and Russia. All Roman Catholic churches have been closed down as places of worship, and nearly all have been completely destroyed inside, only the walls, roof, and tower remaining. Nor have the Protestant churches escaped, with the exception (it would appear to be the only one) of the small German church in Madrid. In that little church divine service still goes on, thanks to the great courage and devotion of the pastor, Dr. Fliedner, and his popularity amongst the poor of Madrid, thanks also to its position (it is very small and is built between houses and behind a garden with trees). The English church in Barcelona has been closed. The two non-conformist places of worship at Clot and Pueblo Nuevo have been burnt. . . .
>
> Visitors to Madrid are shown 'an unburnt church' as a piece of propaganda, and some families in Madrid have had permission to hold private Mass. But these are the loneliest exceptions. . . .

> The lovely churches of Valencia have been burnt out or destroyed inside, and are now used as garages, repair shops, depots, and so on. . . .
>
> In Russia the churches are full and religion is a power still. In Russia persecution has a meaning. In loyalist Spain there is nothing left to persecute. . . .

Religion rather than economics is the key to the Spanish struggle, and religion will determine the issue when the same battle is fought on English soil. It is only the mentally inert who still dismiss the Spanish struggle by repeating a few party slogans. "Anti-clericalism, not anti-religion. . . . Alliance between the materialistic Church and reactionaries. . . ." These phrases are twice blessed, for they absolve both the speaker and his audience from the travail of thought. Let us leave them to their slogans, and search for the significance of this totalitarian fury seeking to destroy in Red Spain every trace of religion, Protestant as well as Catholic.

The war in Spain is only a phase in the recurring battle between two rival interpretations of life, the spiritual and the materialistic. The economic issues are of secondary importance. It is the paradox of Marxian materialism, that the religion Marx rejects provides the only rational basis for the reforms Marx desired. If the evils of capitalism are the consequence not of the evil wills of sinning men, but of predetermined material forces, the indignation with which Marx attacks capitalists is irrational. If the soul be a figment and free will an illusion, and no man more than a machine, it is no more immoral to exploit a wage slave than to exploit a machine, for "morality" has no meaning in a world of machinery. A motor car may be inefficient; it cannot possibly be immoral. If we argue from the Marxian premise it is impossible to prove that it is more immoral to throw discarded workmen into the streets than to sell discarded machinery for scrap iron. Religion alone endows man with moral rights, providing the weak with a charter, and imposing upon the powerful definite obligations to the weak.

We cannot escape the fate of Spain if we fight materialism with materialistic methods. Materialism is an inconsequential doctrine, and we must begin by exposing its fundamental failing. Nothing could be more fatuous than to preach deterministic materialism on one platform and to clamour for "Academic Freedom" on the next. This demand for "Academic Freedom" is one of those partial slogans professorial Communists are expected to exploit in the United States. Communism in practice is more logical than Communism in theory. Denial of free will has led in Russia to its inevitable consequence, the abolition of all freedom.

We must fight materialism with the weapons of the spirit, for Communism cannot be kept at bay merely by social reform, which is not a substitute for, but a logical consequence of, Christianity. The premise that rich men will find it more difficult than the poor to enter the kingdom of heaven is the premise on which a Christian society must be built. Christ did not say, "Don't bother about doctrine, provided you preach socialism." Christ said, "Seek ye first the Kingdom of God, and all these things shall be added unto you." The modern tendency is to reverse the order of importance, and to endeavour to get the man in the street back into the pew by preaching the latest economic fad from the pulpit.

"The determination to provide," said the Dean of Canterbury, "the utmost cultural as well as physical opportunities to all gives promise of the realisation of a social order nearer to the intention of Christ than anything I have seen in Spain during any of my previous visits." But God did not become man only to provide swimming pools and elementary education for the poor.

If I criticize, as I shall, the deans who visited Red Spain, I criticize them because they have betrayed the great traditions of the Church to which they belong. If England is to be recalled to religion the national Church must play her part in that recall. In England and in the United States an attitude of hazy benevolence to Communism is a popular substitute for social service. It costs nothing in money or in time, and helps to establish a reputation for intelligence. It is doubly unfortunate that the Church of England, still enjoying great prestige and power, should be weakened at this critical moment because so many of our leading ecclesiastics speak with vague sympathy and respect of Russian Communism. In so far as these ecclesiastics are moved by sympathy for the poor, their leftist views are praiseworthy, but their sincerity would be less questionable if they endeavoured to apply Communist methods to reduce the grave disproportion between the stipends of the higher and lower clergy in their own Church. The usual explanation of this disparity is not wholly convincing. Episcopal entertaining expenses may be heavy, but a Socialist bishop should be content to offer his guests high tea.

The spell of Red Spain is a symptom less of an increasing interest in social justice than of a failure of nerve. Youth, it is hoped, may be recaptured if the pulpit becomes the loud speaker for leftist doctrines. No more melancholy miscalculation can be conceived. Within a mile of my home there are two Anglo-Catholic churches; in both the Christianity of the Incarnation is preached with courage and sincerity. Both churches are full, but congregations are declining in those churches where preachers who can be distinguished from politicians only by the positions of their collar studs, proclaim the new gospel in which a diluted Christianity is blended with full-blooded Socialism.

There is no need for pessimism. The rapid decline of Anglicanism in the eighteenth century was followed by the Evangelical and Anglo-Catholic revivals, and Anglicanism may yet produce in this century a revival no less remarkable than the revivals associated with the names of Wesley and Keble.

It would be difficult to over-estimate the debt of England to the Anglican Church of the last century. Posterity will not easily find among modern Anglicans men who will rank with the great Victorian divines, with King or Lincoln, Temple, Pusey, Keble, Lightfoot, Church or Farrar. A verger who showed me over Canterbury Cathedral told me that in Dean Farrar's day the police had to control the long queue of would-be worshippers, extending far beyond the Cathedral into the street. "In those days," he said, "they preached the word of God. But this Dean of ours he preaches Social Credit, and there are no queues to worry the police."

The great Victorians doubtless have their successors in the Church of to-day, but they will not be found among those who use their pulpits as sounding boards for revolutionary economic lectures or Left-Wing propaganda.

I wish I knew the answer to a question I was asked during my journey through Spain.

"Your Protestants are Christians, are they not? And if they are Christians surely they must feel that it is shocking to murder thousands of bishops and priests, and particularly shocking to burn so many priests alive. Why are your bishops so eager to scold Mussolini and Hitler, and yet are so slow to condemn the barbarous atrocities on defenceless priests and nuns?"

I wish I had a solution to the selective indignation of certain Protestant ecclesiastics. Anti-clericalism might be pleaded as an excuse for an attack on Cardinal Archbishops, but the priests who have been murdered by the thousands are underpaid and overworked members of the proletariat, themselves of peasant stock.

Europe to-day is facing a threat even more dangerous than the Moslem threat to the Christian world of the Middle Ages and the Renaissance. Constantinople would not have fallen but for the bitter rivalry between the Byzantines who accepted the belated reconciliation with Rome and those who averred that they would rather be Moslems than Latins; Communists may yet capture the Anglo-Saxon world if they continue to enjoy their present success in enlisting the sympathetic support of foolish Christians in their campaign against Christianity.

The case for a United Christian Front was stated by my Father, Sir Henry Lunn, in a letter to *The Times* on July 23, 1937. My Father wrote:

> SIR,—In 1925, as British Treasurer of the Universal Conference of Life and Work, now sitting at Oxford, I was present at the official memorial service held at Stockholm to the martyred Russian Patriarch Tikhon. All Christians united in this expression of their sympathy for the martyrs of Russia and their detestation of the persecutions of which they were the victims. According to the Special Correspondent of the *Manchester Guardian* (June 24, 1937):
>> The attack on religion has been more radical in Loyalist Spain than anywhere else in the world, including even Mexico and Russia. . . . Nor have Protestant Churches escaped. . . . The two non-conformist places of worship at Clot and Pueblo Nuevo have been burnt. . . . In Loyalist Spain there is nothing left to persecute.
>
> Why should Christians to-day be less united in their detestation of persecution than they were in the time of the Russian persecution? Is it because they have been misled into accepting the myth of a military rising against a democratic Government? I know Spain well. I was in Cádiz on the day of the General Election, 1936, and was left with no illusions as to the methods under which that election was held.
>
> At the Methodist Conference in Bradford, which is still sitting, and which represents more than 2,000,000 adherents, the committee of which I was a member drafted a resolution, which was carried unanimously, and which affirmed that the religious situation in Russia, Germany, Spain, and other countries calls for special intercession at the present time, when the universal Church is confronted with a concerted and violent attack upon the faith. It expresses its sorrow at the sufferings of Christians in these countries, deplores the

violence and bloodshed which have accompanied the civil strife in Spain, and prays for the speedy ending of the war.

This resolution wipes out, so far as Methodism is concerned, the tragic disgrace of being involved in the action of the self-appointed committee of six, including two Deans and a leading Methodist minister, who accepted the hospitality of the Government of Valencia and gave a report based exclusively on their visit to the territory governed by Valencia. Such action would have been paralleled in the early history of the Christian Church if six Christians had accepted Nero's hospitality and visited Rome, reporting afterwards to the Church at Jerusalem that Nero promised when affairs were settled to give perfect liberty to the form of Divine Worship which he had driven into the Catacombs.

For fifty years I have been actively associated with the movement for the Reunion of Christendom. We have never worked to reunite Protestants against Rome, but to unite all Christians in the war against anti-Christ. The Reunion Conference at Grindelwald in 1895 commissioned me to convey an address to the Pope in reply to the bull *Ad Anglos*. The address affirmed that "underlying all our differences there was a real unity." It was signed by the Moderator of the Presbyterian Church in England, the Chairman of the Baptist Union, Hugh Price Hughes, the Methodist leader, and notably by Dr. Farrar, subsequently Dean of Canterbury. He would certainly never have anticipated that his successor at Canterbury would broadcast a plea for the Valencia Government from Madrid, when every Catholic Church in that city had been closed by that Government.

Since August 4, 1914, we have been sated with horrors and have lost that power of sympathy to which Robert Wilberforce appealed on behalf of the victims of the Slave Trade and Gladstone on behalf of a comparative handful of suffering Bulgarians. But now the world-wide campaign against Christians calls for united action by all Christian men. Meanwhile:

The souls of them that have been slain for the World of God and for the testimony which they held, cry with a loud voice, saying: "How long, O Lord, holy and true, wilt thou refrain from judging and avenging our blood upon those who dwell on the earth?"

My Father's original resolution was far more definite than the resolution eventually passed. The Methodist minister, referred to in the above letter, seconded the resolution which was carried. My Father did not, of course, mean to imply in his letter that the resolution in question was an implicit vote of censure on the Methodist minister concerned.

My Father has since obtained the enthusiastic support of a number of eminent Anglicans, Methodists and Congregationalists for a public appeal on the lines of his letter. The Archbishop of Westminster replied in a letter as follows:

> Those who belong to the Catholic and Roman Church will have read with appreciation and respect Sir Henry Lunn's moving appeal in your columns for a united Christian Front against the world-wide anti-Christian onslaught. Pius XI explicitly appeals in his letter "Divini Redemptoris" to all who believe in God. Between those who believe in Christ as true God and true man and worship Him there should be charity—an effort to draw nearer to Him and so nearer to one another. This means not only friendly relationship but mutual help in defending the civilization which is founded on the truths enunciated on the Nicene creed. Sir Henry rightly insists on this bond between us. Let us be frank. There have been in the past misunderstandings and faults of manner on both sides, and of temper or a lack of charity in controversy. These, our failings and differences, the enemies of religion have exploited. But the realization of a common peril is drawing Christians together in practical sympathy. In Germany prayers have been offered in Catholic churches for the persecuted Protestants, and in this country the Methodists have unanimously approved the resolution of sympathy for the persecuted Catholics in Spain. I thank them and Sir Henry Lunn with all my heart.

The concluding passage of this letter in which the Archbishop refutes the charge that the Vatican sympathizes with Fascism will be quoted in a subsequent chapter.

10 THE *TE DEUM* OF THE DEAN

> "*A real religious note lies behind life in Spain to-day.*"
> The Dean of Canterbury.

> "*Under the twelve months' administration of the present Spanish Government more than 4000 priests have been murdered . . . nuns have been stripped naked in the streets, outraged and murdered; churches, shrines, private chapels and religious statues have been desecrated and destroyed. The Cathedral of Valencia, the seat of the Government, has had a road driven through it. . . .*"
> The Times, April 16, 1937.

> "*Someone is financing the tour, of course, but the less said about that the better.*"
> The Dean of Canterbury.

NATIONALIST SPAIN will not easily forget that two clerical deputations have visited unredeemed Spain where the churches are closed, but no clerical deputation has shown any interest in reconquered Spain where the churches are open.

It was not only the partiality displayed by the clerical deputations that shocked Nationalist Spain, but certain details to which the Nationalists attached, perhaps, an altogether disproportionate importance. They were shocked that clergymen should accept travelling and other expenses from a Government in whose territory priests had been massacred and the churches burned. They were amused rather than shocked that the clerics accepted with alacrity the advice given them by their hosts to leave their clerical collars behind them in England. A courteous guest complies with the wishes of his host in trivial matters, and I do not think that the travelling clerics can be blamed for discarding those clerical collars which might have led to a regrettable confusion between progressive deans who accept the hospitality of a Government in whose territory Christians are persecuted, and reactionary priests who *are willing to die* for Christianity.

The Spaniards are unreasonable in such matters. They argue with conviction that though a soldier might discard his uniform to escape in disguise from captivity, or to penetrate as a spy into enemy lines, and that though a soldier of Christ might sneak round Madrid disguised as a proletarian while he was saying Mass at the risk of his life, no soldier, whether of the King, or of the King of Kings, should accept the hospitality of those who have insulted his uniform and who have done all in their power to banish that uniform from the territory under their control.

The first clerical deputation to Red Spain included the Dean of Rochester, the Dean of Chichester, the Rev. Philip Usher, Chaplain to the Bishop of Gloucester, Mr. Percy Bartlet of the Society of Friends (what would Fox have thought of fraternizing with those who preach a doctrine of violence and hate?), the Rev. Henry Brinton, and the Rev. Henry Carter. According to Mr. Carter the party were the "guests of the Government of Spain." Mr. Carter is a distinguished Methodist, but his sympathy for the Red Government survived the discovery that Methodists were not allowed to meet for public worship in Barcelona.

In their report the deputation assert that priests were seldom killed by their own parishoners, unless they were "actively unpopular." If this be true, the martyrs of Spain will receive rather a cool welcome from St. Peter, for there is nothing more disedifying than a shepherd who is unpopular with his sheep.

From Barcelona the deputation proceeded to Madrid, where it seems many deservedly unpopular priests have been executed. Mr. Henry Carter recalls "two unforgettable memories" associated with the day they entered Madrid. The first is that of Dr. Underhill leading the little delegation in the *Te Deum* and a psalm just before they entered the city. "As I write," says Mr. Carter, "I seem to stand in that chill dawn and hear the words 'Thou shalt not be afraid of the terror that flyeth by night.'" But there was nothing to be afraid of; they were not wearing their clerical collars.

The *Te Deum*, according to tradition, was first sung when St. Ambrose was besieged in his Basilica by the army of an heretical Emperor. If, however, the *Te Deum* is to be sung by Protestants entering a city where every church is closed and every decent priest is in hiding, it had better be revised. "The ignoble army of martyrs disedify thee" would bring the *Te Deum* into line with modern thought.

The second of Mr. Carter's "unforgettable memories" was provided by an hotel keeper who refused to accept payment for the party, a generous gesture, but not perhaps surprising if the Government of Spain, as Mr. Carter elsewhere assures us, were paying the expenses of the party. The inn-keeper could hardly expect to be paid twice over. But Mr. Carter was deeply moved. "With a vivid sense of the presence of God and the chivalry of man we rejoined our colleagues," he proclaimed.

I prefer Mr. Carter's disarming candour on the question of hospitality to the more oblique references of a latter visitor, the Dean of Canterbury, whose cryptic allusion to expense is quoted at the head of this chapter.

I spent some time in Spain trying to convince Spaniards that the Barcelona deputation does not represent the Church of England. I quoted as much as I could remember of the Anglican Bishop of Gibraltar's protest. The Bishop stated that had he been consulted he would have advised this deputation "to visit both sides, and not to go as the guests of either party," and he adds, "I must protest that their report is wholly inadequate as an account of 'alleged atrocities' against the Church in Spain. I have visited Spain each year for four years. I have seen a progressive deterioration of the organs of government during this period, and witnessed the burning of the historic Church at Niebla last April (1936)—one of the several hundreds of buildings wantonly destroyed under the eyes of the authorities. . . . The Churchmen's Mission does not represent the Anglican Church nor the diocese of Gibraltar."

The Duke of Argyll, Abbot Martin, the Rev. H. J. Fynes-Clinton, the Rev. W. R. Corbould are the signatories to a letter concluding with the following paragraph:

> We believe that we represent the feelings of countless English church people, especially the Catholic-minded clergy and laity, of shame for this sympathy being shown with the Red enemies of the Church, the suppression of facts; and of our admiration and gratitude for the faithful and splendid stand that is being taken by His Holiness the Pope and the Roman Catholic Church against the common enemy of civilisation and Christendom.

Sir Francis Lindley reacted with equal vigour against the attitude expressed in the report of the clerical deputation to Red Spain.

> The attitude of some of our highly-placed divines is stupefying, and to me personally, as a life-long member of the Church of England, revolting. The ineptitude of those English clerics who embark on the sea of foreign affairs is, of course, notorious; no one should have been surprised when they worked overtime to advocate a policy to lead inevitably to the total subjugation of Abyssinia, . . . but I have cudgelled my brains in vain to find the explanation of their support of the so-called Government of Spain. I hesitate to accept the only logical explanation that they do not regard the Catholic Church as a branch of Christianity, or professing Roman Catholics as entitled to the rights enjoyed by the rest of mankind.

11 THE INCONVENIENT DEAD

"And ye shall be hated of all men for my name's sake. . . ."
St. Matthew, XI, 22–25.

Nothing could have been more inconsiderate than the carelessness of the Red Government. Every reasonable man will understand their difficulty in preventing the wholesale massacre of priests who were so deservedly unpopular with their parishioners, but they should have insisted on a fair trial after a *prima facie* case of unpopularity had been established. They would not have had any difficulty in manufacturing the necessary evidence to prove that these priests had been wicked enough to defend their churches (a Fascist thing to do) or had used their confessionals as ammunition dumps. In this case every reasonable Progressive in England would have been satisfied, but the Spaniards were careless and lazy, and did not take the trouble.

This makes things difficult for their supporters, the Duchess of Atholl, the Dean of Canterbury, the Dean of Rochester and the Dean of Chichester trying so hard to represent Azaña as a sort of Spanish Gladstone, his Cabinet as a kind of National Government, and Largo Caballero as a genial Lansbury, with little help from the Valencia Government. Every decent person would have been ready to make allowances for the noble rage of a democracy threatened by a military rebellion. The legal execution of a few score priests, the murder of perhaps a few hundred, could have been explained as an excess of otherwise justified anti-clericalism. But there is a way of doing these things that the Red Government has not mastered. According to the highest ecclesiastical authority in Spain about 14,000 priests and monks have been murdered, some of them after cruel physical torture.

The new apologetics, conducted by Christians on behalf of a Government which has murdered Christians, is ingenious. The defence is based on three pleas. The first line of defence is to defame the dead; the priests would not have been killed if they hadn't been unpopular. A priest was killed by his own people only if he was actively unpopular. If he was popular the agreeable task of removing him was left to marauding bands of Anarchists and Communists.

"The hatred," continues the report, "was much more violent against the religious orders than against the parochial clergy." "If the religious orders are distrusted," wrote Professor Allison Peers in the *Church Times* some years ago, "it is not by the poor, the sick or the hungry." Professor Peers is recognised as one of the greatest modern authorities in Spain. His book, *The Spanish Tragedy*, has been praised as the most scholarly and objective study of the period immediately preceding the civil war. As an Anglican, he will not be suspected of bias in his generous tributes to the Spanish Church. He states that outside the ranks of professed anti-clericals he has entirely failed to observe any such deeply rooted distrust as their enemies declare they inspire.

The second line of defence is to misrepresent the motive of the persecution. Apologists for Red Spain insist that the persecution of religion in Red Spain is inspired not by hatred of religion, but by anti-clericalism.

Professor Peers writes:

> For that it is religion in every form known to them, that the Reds are persecuting, no one who has followed the history of Spain during the last few years with knowledge and understanding can possibly doubt. I am aware that the group of Churchmen who visited two cities of Spain last winter "found no evidence of an organized godless propaganda, and were unable, on inquiry, to hear of any caricatures of God, of Christ, or of the Virgin and Saints. There is much that could be said about this, but the most obvious thing is that they could not have looked very far. Even the respectable caricaturist, Bagaría, whose former newspaper was so moderate in its Republicanism that its enemies among the Left extremists used to say it had been bought by the Jesuits, has begun to amuse himself, in the Barcelona *Vanguardia*, by representing God the Father in a way as humourless as it is irreverent. As for the articles and caricatures in the extremist papers, there is enough of the anti-God movement in them to fill a volume. During the last two decades, I have seen anti-clericalism develop from an idiosyncrasy into a tendency, and from a tendency into a movement. I have seen the anti-clerical movement widen its scope and grow into an anti-God movement, in which, it is true, anti-clericalism is still the most conspicuous feature, but is clearly recognizable (if I may quote the title of a most revealing article recently published in *Solidaridad Obrera*, and referred to in the *Universe*) as the mask which hides the anti-God face. If the Reds should win, the mask will surely and immediately be removed and the evolution of the anti-God movement will be complete.

Even more striking is the testimony of the Reds, who have a disconcerting habit of contradicting their own supporters. Well-meaning clerical deputations issue their solemn reports, and do everything in their power to prove that these democratic Reds are very fond of God but not at all fond of priests. This would be much more convincing had not the Reds anticipated them by explaining that they serve out this sort of misinformation for the benefit of innocent dupes. Here is an extract from *Solidaridad Obrera* for January 28, 1937. This paper is the organ of the Regional Confederation of Labour in Catalonia, and the mouthpiece of the Spanish National Confederation of Labour.

> It appears that Alvarez del Vayo found himself obliged in the League of Nations to define the limits of our revolution. "Spain will have," he said, "a social democracy and therefore have freedom of religion." Admirable. We know the value of words used by diplomatists if spoken in Geneva meetings.
>
> Lenin said that religion was opium. He did not say enough. Opium stupefies, enervates. Little by little it robs man of his organic energies, but it does not go beyond animal physiology.
>
> We do not know up to what point we can speak of the "freedom of religion". . . . The "freedom for evil" is an excessively liberal principle.
>
> If we do not allow the freedom of drunkenness, prostitution, suicide, must we allow fanaticism?
>
> It is enough to judge religion by the simple fact of its burnt churches. Not one remains standing, not an effigy remains intact. Hardly a shred remains. With all this they still have pretentions of returning to the Faith. . . .
>
> This speech of Alvarez del Vayo with his kind of promise or compromise, that Spain will re-establish the Catholic religion, may have sounded very good in the League of Nations. It appears to have given tone to the discussion; but here in Spain it makes us smile.

The third method is to defame the Spanish Church as rich, corrupt, and friend of reactionaries. These charges shall receive a detailed reply in the next chapter.

12 THE SPANISH CHURCH

CERTAIN FACTS about the Spanish Church need to be affirmed and reaffirmed. First, Spain is overwhelmingly a Catholic country. Protestants in Spain are scarcely more numerous than members of the Greek Orthodox Church in England. If every Anglican or Nonconformist Church in Great Britain were burned or closed, and a few Greek Orthodox churches left open for propaganda purposes, it would be difficult to convince an intelligent foreigner that Great Britain was not the scene of a violent anti-Christian persecution.

Secondly, no Protestant has been molested by the Nationalists because of his religion. Mr. Archibald Ramsay, a Presbyterian and a Member of Parliament, writes as follows in *The Times*:[1]

> I received to-day a categorical assurance from an unimpeachable source, with General Franco's full authority, to the effect that under his régime complete toleration of religious practice and education is to be extended to Protestants in Spain as and when he can make this regulation effective.

[1] July 28, 1937.

As a proof I am further informed by the same authority that the Protestant school and church in Salamanca have in the last week or two been handed back to Protestant hands and complete liberty of action extended to them.

The national Church in Spain has been, on the evidence of the *Manchester Guardian* correspondent, the victim of a persecution more ruthless, more violent and more thorough than any religious persecution in modern times.

If the ratio of apostates in Red Spain equalled a certain historic ratio of one in twelve there would have been thousands of apostates available to escort deans and duchesses round the territory where deans and duchesses have been murdered. But the number of such priests can be counted not by the thousand, not by the hundred, not by the score.

The dissident Basque priesthood raises a different problem. They have been disowned by their hierarchy, and they are in no sense representative of Basque Catholicism. Only a minority of Basques are fighting against Franco, and many, perhaps most, of these are Left-Wing extremists. The British public, deceived in this as in so many other matters by Red propaganda, were much surprised to discover that the majority of the Bilbao children (devout Catholics for propaganda purposes) greeted their English hosts with the clenched fist of the Communist salute.

Of the four Basque provinces, Navarre and Alava were solidly behind Franco from the first. Guipuzco was divided, and even in the independent republic of Vizcaya there were many Basques who seized the first opportunity to desert to Franco.

In Red Spain the bishops and priests have died like heroes. Hundreds of them have been offered their lives if they would deny Christ, and they have preferred death, often death by torture. The whole Chapter of Toledo with exception of one canon (fifty-six in all) were slaughtered. Not one parish priest is alive in the four Catalán provinces.

Eleven Bishops have been martyred, some of them burnt alive. According to the highest ecclesiastical authority in Spain, more than ten thousand priests and monks have been murdered. Thousands of nuns have been assassinated and outraged.

The persecution in Red Spain has enriched the Christian martyrology with stories of courage such as those to come down to us from the first century of the Christian era. I owe this story to the Roman Catholic Bishop of Gibraltar:

A priest was being led out to his death. He was bound. As he faced the executioners he said, "I want to bless you. Please free my hands."

A Red cut the ropes and then hacked off his hands.

"Bless us now," he sneered.

And the priest did bless them, moving about his bleeding stumps until he died.

It is easy from the comfort and security of English deaneries to defame the Church that produced men such as this, but it must be difficult even for the most prejudiced to believe that those who killed such priests were inspired by an enlightened anti-clericalism.

Only the ungenerous minority of invincible bigots will withhold their admiration from the martyrs of Spain, but there are many people, misled by Red propaganda, who sincerely believe that the Spanish Church invited this persecution.

The Church in Spain has been represented as rich in the midst of grinding poverty, as the ally of reaction and as the enemy of progress. The wealth of the Church is a propaganda myth, for the Church has been the victim of a long series of partial and complete confiscations in the years 1812, 1820, 1835, 1837, 1868 and 1931.

The State, having expropriated and disendowed the Church, agreed to pay the stipends of the clergy. Anglicans who have attacked the wealth of the Spanish Church will be consoled to discover that the Primate of Spain receives an income of roughly one-tenth that of the Primate of Great Britain, and that there are very few Bishops in Spain whose stipends exceed a quarter of those paid to Anglican Bishops.

Let us take 1913, the last year before the War, when England was on gold, and the value of the peseta more stable, as a basis of comparison. In 1913 the Primate of Spain received the equivalent of about £1600 a year, and the Bishop of Madrid £1100. Eight Bishops were paid at the rate of £400. Of all the parish priests, only fifty received an annual grant of £100. Three thousand, four hundred and ninety-five received annual stipends varying from £20 to £25 a year. Additional sources of revenue, such as Mass offerings, very rarely exceeded, and were often considerably less in the aggregate than the official stipend. Spanish priests were overworked and underpaid members of the proletariat.

When the Republic was proclaimed in 1931 almost its first act was to confiscate such Church property as the Church had accumulated since the last spoliation, and to make it clear that in the future the State would pay no further stipends to the clergy, stipends paid previously by the State, not as an act of charity, but as an act of justice. The new blow was peculiarly mean, because many of the Spanish priests had been persuaded to vote for the Republic on the plea that that State would reduce the stipends paid to the higher clergy, and increase the stipends paid to the parish priests. More than a century has passed since the first disendowment of the Church, and in the course of this century the Church has gradually acquired property. It is the poor who have benefited by these new endowments, for the Church has educated more than half of those who have received education, and has been responsible nation-wide for hospitals and other works of charity. These charities cost money, and it is clear that the Church must have acquired funds subsequent to its spoliation. These funds came largely from religious who entered religious Orders. Young girls would bring dowries with them, and resign in favour of the Orders any rights to moneys they might subsequently inherit. Furthermore, just as charitable people in this country will bequeath or give money to hospitals or schools, so in Spain they would bequeath or give money to the Church; they knew that a very small proportion of money would go towards overhead expenses, and that the Church could be trusted to administer economically the charities it controlled. To describe the Church as "rich," however, is misleading. A trustee is not regarded as rich merely because he administers the estate of a millionaire. The Spanish ecclesiastics were the underpaid trustees of national charity.

The spoliation of the Church has never been a popular movement in Spain. The Spanish people are realists, and discovered early in the last century that it was the poor who suffered when the Church was despoiled, and the rich Liberals who benefited. A father who has given his daughter a dowry when she joins a convent, very naturally regards as robbers those who confiscate that dowry along with the other endowments of the convent in question. Spaniards who benefited directly or indirectly from the charitable work of the Church, did not share the enthusiasm of British Progressives regarding the transfer of money from the Church to the politicians.

During the last century Liberalism has dominated Spanish politics. Spanish Liberalism has always been anti-clerical, and the property of the Church has provided an outlet for the instincts of looting.

"Everything has just disappeared," exclaimed the Duke of Rivas after one of the early spoliations. "The army has not been increased by one battalion, nor the navy by even a barge, nor has the lot of the proletariat been improved."

The record of Liberal Governments in Spain so far as

education is concerned has been a record of destruction. The Church was prevented from teaching, and no adequate substitute was provided. In the middle of the nineteenth century the State sonorously proclaimed itself as solely responsible for education, but it did little to implement these loud claims; most of the actual teaching was done by and at the expense of the religious orders. They educated more than one-half of those who required education. They did a great deal, and now are attacked because they did not do more. Liberals did very little and expect to be judged not by their record but by their professions.

"Backward as Spain has long been in this respect," writes Professor Allison Peers, "it is hardly possible to imagine in what condition she would be were it not for the labours of the clergy, in particular, the religious Orders." Professor Peers has described the work of these Orders in a series of interesting articles. He quoted the puzzled exclamation of a former pupil of an Augustinian college.

> How can we explain the apparently meaningless hatred of the religious Orders which seems to inspire some of our politicians? Have they not laboured, and do they not labour, ceaselessly and freely, in the interests of Spanish culture, both in Spain and abroad? Is the work of these scholars, critics, educators and missionaries nothing but a pious legend? Do not these literary and scientific works and institutions really exist—these books, in particular, of which the importance and value have been recognized again and again by men whose ideas are completely opposed to those of their authors? Are not these colleges, laboratories, libraries, reviews—above all, these thousands upon thousands of pupils and students who have benefited from them—palpable realities? And if we are told that no objection is taken to them as individuals, and they are only to be expelled from Spain because they are members of communities which are thought to be undesirable, is not the reply that, as individuals, they could never have done the great work which they have accomplished, for only when they are

organized as a community does it become practically and economically possible?"

It is well said, and, to a reasonable and unprejudiced person, I think it will seem unanswerable.

Professor Peers pays a striking tribute to the Brothers of the Christian Schools. He writes:

"The majority of the Brothers' schools are situated in the poorer quarters of the great cities, in towns where little other elementary education is to be found, or in mining districts where the population is dense over a comparatively small area. Many of the schools have been established by private benefaction, others by industrial concerns which would hardly be accused of sentimentalism. . . . Brothers of the people, indeed, are these; their work brings neither to themselves nor to their Orders any such great distinction as comes to the scholars of other religious Orders, but it forms a firm foundation of charity and devotion without which Spain would be immeasurably poorer."

The Church in Spain is hated not for its defects but for its virtues. Anti-clericalism in Spain, as Mr. Douglas Woodruff has justly said, is not the fruit of irritation with supine and hypocritical wealth. "It is," he writes, "the hatred of men who want to impose one set of secular doctrines against those who stand in their path and maintain by example and precept another doctrine and a wholly different view of the purpose of life and the nature of man."

"The Spanish Church," writes Professor Peers, "is credited by its enemies with being over-powerful and over-rich. But its true power and its true riches are of the kind that no man can take from it: the millions who worship with an intensity and a regularity hard to parallel and the thousands who live saintly lives of devotion."

That Spanish Catholics should support the Nationalists who are fighting to save Christian Spain is not surprising, but it is absurd to deduce from this or from other facts that the Vatican is committed to the support of Fascism. On this question the authoritative pronouncement of the Archbishop of Westminster will command respect. I quote the concluding passage of a letter to *The Times;* the opening passage has already been quoted in another connection.

> May I take this occasion of replying to ill-informed critics who represent the Church as the secret ally of Fascism. Such persons cannot know the pronouncements of the Popes during the last fifty years. The Church as such is not concerned with political systems, and the Vatican maintains relations with any State which permits Catholics to worship unmolested and to give a Catholic education to their children. The Pope, who was represented at the Coronation of our King George VI, has spoken and speaks frequently of Great Britain in terms of the deepest affection and respect. Those who deduce from the fact that his relations are no less amicable with the Italian State, that the Vatican has any special preference for Fascism, should reflect that the Vatican has not broken off relations with Valencia in favour of Burgos, that the relations between the Vatican and Nazi Germany are very strained, and that the influence of the Catholic hierarchy in Belgium has been exercised against the Belgian form of Fascism (Rexists).
>
> In conclusion, I plead for 'sound words,' for the use of terms in a defined consistent sense. Pius XI, who so strongly condemns totalitarianism, is most unjustly identified with any form thereof; it is a gross fallacy and a cruel one to dub all those who are opposed to atheistic Communism as Fascists or Nazis. Let us have straight thinking, and in all things charity.

Nobody denies that Spanish Catholics have always regarded Spanish Liberalism with profound distrust. Nor is this surprising, for Liberalism in Spain has never concealed its hostility to the Church, and few institutions co-operate with their declared enemies. It would be as reasonable to attack the Jews for their very natural hostility to Nazi Germany as to criticize the Spanish Church for her reluctance to support Spanish Liberalism.

And yet human nature is invincibly sanguine. Thousands of priests voted for the Republic in 1931 for reasons I have already mentioned. The Papal Nuncio, Monsignor Tedeschini, and the Spanish hierarchy accepted the Republic in 1931 with an optimism proved by subsequent events to be tragically mistaken. Even when the Republic resumed the traditional Liberal policy of spoliation and suppression, they still made every effort to work within the framework of the new Constitution for the victory of parties friendly to the Church. It was the refusal of the Church to identify herself with reaction that provoked the anti-clericalism of the Right.

"I'm a Catholic but I'm violently anti-clerical," a distinguished Spaniard recently remarked to me. "All this trouble is due to the Church. The Church was so consiliatory to the Left, so anxious to work with the Republic, that it never gave Spain a clear lead against the Red peril. Many foolish priests voted Republican in 1931, because the Republicans assured them that they would raise their salaries. The Pope, would you believe it, still recognizes the Madrid Government, and still fails to recognize Burgos. We have had Papal Nuncios here who were little better than Socialists."

"I am an anti-clerical," said another Spaniard, "because our ecclesiastics have lost a due sense of the dignity of their position. The Cardinal Archbishop of Toledo, who is the Primate of Spain, wrote a personal letter to the self-styled President of the Basque Republic, appealing to him to break away from the Madrid Government. If he had to write to that sort of person, he ought to have got one of his minor canons to sign the letter."

The truth is, that the Church in Spain, like the Church elsewhere, has been prepared to co-operate with any government willing to guarantee freedom of worship and Christian education for the young. Nobody denies that the Church in Spain, like the Church of England, had it defects.

Its policy, like the policy of other Churches, has not always been wise, but when Mussolini accused Anglican prelates of being quicker to detect the mote that is in their brother's eye than the beam in their own, he was voicing a popular continental criticism of smugness, that most characteristic British failing. Anglicans who complacently criticize the alleged alliance between the Church in Spain and the ruling powers expose themselves to a crushing retort which they ignore.

> The Church of England [writes Dean Inge] has been freely accused of too great complaisance to the powers that be, when those powers were oligarchic. Some of the clergy are now trying to repeat rather than redress this error by an obsequious attitude to King Working-man. . . . The taunt of Helen to Aphrodite in the third book of the *Iliad* sounds very apposite when we read the speeches of some clerical 'Christian Socialists' who find it more exciting to organize processions of the unemployed than to attend to their professional duties. "Go and sit thou by his side and depart from the way of the gods; neither let thy feet ever bear thee back to Olympus; but still be vexed for his sake, and guard him till he make thee his wife, or rather his slave."
>
> It is as a slave and not as an honoured help-mate that the Social Democrats would treat any Christian body that helped them to overthrow our present civilization.

Human motives are always mixed, and it is of our most creditable motives that we are most conscious. Few men are cynical in the choice of a political creed, and the tendency of ecclesiastics to swim comfortably with the Left-Wing stream is only partially explained in the passage that I have quoted from Dr. Inge. It would be no less unfair to suggest that ecclesiastics are influenced by the fact that progressive views are no disqualification for ecclesiastical promotion. A certain blindness to the sufferings of the poor in Victorian England or to the sufferings of the Church in modern Spain, cannot be explained by the easy formula: "There are none so blind as those who want Sees."

A report published in a recent book, *Men, Money and Ministry: A Plea for Economic Reform in the Church of England*, is signed by many Bishops. The Report says, "The sources of income do not command moral assent. Ninety-nine per cent of the miners in the country disapprove of mining royalties. Every miner in the north-east of England knows that the largest share of mining royalties in the north-east goes to the Ecclesiastical Commission. . . ."

The Report mentions the gross disproportion between the stipends of the higher and lower clergy and the tithe problem. Now let us suppose that a "Popular Front" came into power in England and exploited the indignation of the tithe payers, and that, as a result, eleven Anglican Bishops and four thousand of the clergy were murdered and hundreds of churches burned. What should we think of a party of Irish Catholics who, on their return from a hasty visit to England, smugly assured their fellow-countrymen that these excesses were not due to hatred of religion but to anti-clericalism?

The Church of England is to-day almost the only representative in the world of a national Church still mediaeval both in wealth and in political power. It preserves the tithes and endowments and the privileged position of the mediæval territorial Church. Nothing, therefore, could have been more inept than the attacks levelled by certain Anglican dignitaries against the Church in Spain.

13 THE CHARGES AGAINST THE RED TROOPS

"As far as I can see," said my friend, "there's nothing to choose between the Spanish Nationalists and the Reds in this matter of atrocities."

"But how far can you see?" I asked, "and how far have you tried to see?"

If the Black Death which devastated mediæval Europe returned, and if London were decimated by the Plague, and Sussex comparatively immune, a man who remarked glibly, "In this matter of plague, there is nothing to choose between the health statistics of Middlesex and Sussex," would be swept aside as an ignoramus. We are realistic about physical disease because we believe in the body; we are incurious and ineffective about spiritual disease because it is unfashionable to believe in sickness of the soul.

The Red Death, spreading like a plague over modern Europe, is far more devastating in its effects than the Black Death of the fourteenth century, because it has not been diagnosed properly. Accurate diagnosis is a prerequisite to scientific cure, and impossible if we begin by denying the existence of the disease.

No scientific approach to the pathological problem of Communism is possible unless we are prepared to face disagreeable facts, and approach those facts without attempting to conciliate the mental fashion of the day. Snobbery influences our attitude, and it is fashionable to affect a broad detachment towards atrocities and to seek refuge from a complicated problem in facile formulæ.

"Moral Indignation, Its Cause and Cure," was a theme once proposed by Oscar Wilde as suitable for a sociological treatise, a witty crystallization of the *fin-de-siècle* attitude towards moral evil. In the nineties it was modish to register acute distress in the presence of physical ugliness, an unlovely building or a tasteless picture, whereas the correct reaction to moral ugliness was an attitude of cynical detachment. Moral indignation is as rational as æsthetic indignation, and has a therapeutic value as a stimulus, for unless our comatose countrymen can be provoked into hard thinking on the subject of Communism, the tragedy of Spain may be re-enacted in England.

My object at the moment is not to provoke moral indignation, but to stimulate the scientific study of the most interesting social phenomenon of our age, the effect of Communist propaganda on a country.

The atrocity research that I am anxious to promote, has much in common with psychical research. The investigator is faced with the same difficulty of discovering the substratum of fact beneath the layers of fraud, propaganda, deliberate lying, hysteria and malobservation. Unless he is endowed with an authentic scientific curiosity that is undaunted in the search for truth by the distasteful masks truth so often wears, he had better abandon this form of research. Those who have the courage to continue their investigations will be rewarded in psychical and in atrocity research by the discovery and establishment of truths of considerable value to the philosopher and to the social historian.

The atrocities that concern us in this investigation may be classified broadly as follows:

(1) Deterrent executions—executions without due process of trial intended to intimidate a hostile population or a hostile section of a friendly population.

(2) Reprisal executions, motivated by revenge for atrocities, real or alleged, committed by the other side.

(3) Terroristic massacres.

(4) Sadism, that is, cruelty for the sake of cruelty, torture, mutilation, etc., and executions not by shooting, but by burning alive, etc.

Deterrent executions are born of fear, as for example, when a small invading force shoots hostages in order to intimidate *franc-tireurs,* but the terroristic massacre is not directed against those who are regarded as potential assassins of *franc-tireurs,* but against defenceless victims, women, old men, or priests. A terroristic massacre is, as we shall see in due course, a recognised method advocated by Communists for the establishment of a Red Dictatorship.

The case against the Reds is that, whereas deterrent executions and reprisal executions are characteristic of most wars, terroristic massacres and sadism on a large scale are vitually unknown in wars between civilised powers, but are associated with all Communist outbreaks, whether in Russia, or for the brief period of Communist rule in Bavaria, in Hungary during the Bela Kun régime, in Mexico, or in Red Spain.

Our next task is to classify the evidence on which our conclusions must be based.

Witnesses may be divided into three classes:

(1) Friendly witnesses who are or who once were strongly biased in favour of those whom they now charge with atrocities.

(2) Neutrals with no bias.

(3) Unfriendly witnesses with an obvious bias against those accused of atrocities.

It is easy to prove the case against the Reds without calling any witness from those who were among the declared supporters of Franco at the beginning of the Civil War.

Men who have been extravagantly praised by our progressive Press in the days when they were the leaders of the Left, have been driven by sheer horror of the Red Terror into the opposition camp. Men like the late Dr. Miguel de Unamuno, Rector of Salamanca, the opposite number in Spain to Liberal University teachers like Professor Gilbert Murray; N. Alcalá Zamora, President when the Popular Front assumed power; Salvador S. de Madariaga, one of the leading Spanish Liberals; Dr. Gregorio Marañón, President of the Academy of Medicine at Madrid, imprisoned as a Radical under Primo de Rivera; and Alejandro García Lerroux, the doyen of Spanish Radicals, the Lloyd George of Spain, and a former Premier of the Spanish Republic, have all testified to the truth.

Lerroux records the fact that the Red Terror took an even heavier toll of Radicals than of priests, and writes as follows:

> Twenty centuries of Christianity, forty centuries of civilization and progress, have not yet been able to raise the morale or improve the intellectual standing of a whole class of men. That class has been poisoned in modern times by an indigestion of doctrines that prove incomprehensible to their primitive intelligence, and unassimilable by them in their low stage of culture, deadened as their intellects have been and their nature rendered dull by the selfish indifference of the privileged classes. This sorry human beast, abandoned by God and man, on finding himself free can only sting and use his venom like a viper.

No less impressive than the evidence of this converted Radical is the testimony of Cornelius Vanderbilt, whose *Farewell to Fifth Avenue* is a brilliant attack on the New York aristocracy into which he was born. Cornelius

Vanderbilt is often accused of Communistic leanings. Be that as it may, nobody would accuse him of any sympathy with Fascism or the Catholic Church.

> One night at Palou, near Barcelona [he wrote in the American weekly, *Liberty*], I heard a howling mob around a bend in the road. A few minutes later there came straggling down the roadway a tattered rabble, brandishing sticks and knives and rusty rifles. Some of them were bellowing the 'Internationale.' With them were two oxen, and behind the oxen, chained and roped together, were three or four cowled monks, one of whom they had already beheaded. . . . Once I saw two monks who had already been crucified. Their faces were twisted as if the pain had been unbearable. Large railroad spikes had been driven through their shrivelled stomachs, and dried blood covered their legs. . . . At Molins del Rey, I saw a lot of tonsured monks being carried in a manure wagon pulled by a raving mob of ragged boys and girls, mind you, through the village streets. Running along beside the wagon were little girls with pointed sticks which they savagely jabbed into the monks' flesh. At Marquina, held by the Governmentalists, I saw nuns shackled to one another's ankles being dragged by lively mules through the cobblestone streets, the whole tops of their heads ablaze. I was told they had been dipped in kerosene and touched off with long, white church tapers.

Horace W. Abrams, photographer for the Keystone View Company, contributes this picture along with others: "I also photographed a little girl. The Reds chopped off her leg by the thigh because they found out her father was fighting with the rebels. You can guess what they did to the mother, who was quite young. She died."

Neither *The New York Times* nor its correspondent is sympathetic to Fascism, and the evidence of Joseph Lee Mason, writing in *The New York Times* of September 13, 1936, is therefore impressive.

> As we passed the parish church (at El Saucejo), we saw the body of the priest, Father José de la Cora, crucified, head

down, on the main door. The body was clad in ceremonial vestments. The body of his brother, Ramón de la Cora, was lying in front of the church door. He had been shot dead by the Communists. . . . While accompanying a patrol searching houses in Almorgén, we found three nuns of the Carmelite Order in a house that had been ransacked by the Communists. Two of the nuns were dead. The third, Madre Rosa, was alive, but her face had been slashed with knives. . . . At Almorgén was also found an insurgent soldier who had been held a prisoner by the Communists. Both of his eyes had been gouged out, his face was slashed and his fingers had been cut off.

Red atrocities were the cause, rather than the consequence, of the Franco rising; the outrages were not isolated and unplanned but general and continuous. The evidence cited in support is the evidence of British eyewitnesses such as the chairman of the British Residents Emergency Committee in Madrid, and the uncensored despatches of a fair and unbiased *Times* correspondent in Madrid, who is quoted again and again. Crucifixion, soaking in petrol and burning alive of men, women and children, are the routine of Communist terrorism. The case against the Reds in this matter of atrocities is proved long before we need appeal to the official reports issued by the Burgos Government.

Certain conclusions emerge from a study of the Red terror. The brutality of the Roman world into which Christ was born, is returning. Torture, slowly disappearing from a world influenced but never dominated by the Christian ethos, is reappearing, and it is no coincidence that this recrudescence of sadism should coincide with outbursts of that Communism which is directed by the only State to have adopted militant atheism as its creed.

People who like to assure us that "it does not matter what a man believes provided that he is kind" are beginning to wonder whether people will continue to be kind after they have ceased to believe. Events in Spain suggest a somewhat closer connection between creed and code than the moralizing agnostics of the Victorian age were prepared to concede. García Oliver, Minister of Justice in the Government of Valencia, said at a public meeting:[1]

"Man comes not from God but from the beasts; that is why his reactions are those of a beast."

García Oliver is more scientific than the amiable sceptics in England who evade the logical conclusions of their creed.

"Why punish prostitution when it should be legally organized?"

Quite so, and as the Dean of Canterbury remarked, "the determination to provide the utmost cultural as well as physical opportunity to all, gives promise of the realization of a social order nearer to the intention of Christ than anything I have seen in Spain during any of my previous visits." And this is how García Oliver proposes to carry Christ's intentions into effect.

"The courts of Justice are not to be merely popular, but primitive tribunals."

But, of course, as the Dean of Canterbury remarked, "It does not matter what they say with their lips, it is what they mean in their hearts."

The meeting at which García Oliver delivered himself of these views was presided over by the Minister of Propaganda. But it would seem that a verbatim report of the meeting was not considered suitable propaganda for itinerant clerics.

Well may Sir Arthur Bryant exclaim, "Red Spain is not a constitutional democracy. It is an inferno. Since last July some 350,000 non-combatant men, women and children, living helpless in that corner of the Iberian peninsula subject to the rule of what is euphemistically called the Valencia Government, have been butchered in cold blood under conditions of indescribable horror."

---

[1] Reported in *El Diluvio*, January 1, 1937.

Even if every charge against the Nationalists could be proved, it would still be necessary on two vital issues to draw the sharpest distinction between the Nationalists and the Reds. First there is the question of motive. Nationalists execute individuals if proved guilty of crimes, but are not waging war on any particular class of society. The Nationalist army is democratic in the proper sense of the term, for it includes representatives of *every* social class from aristocracy to proletarians and peasants. The Reds, on the other hand, advocate class war, and have put into practice the first postulate of the Marxist revolution, the liquidation of the aristocracy and bourgeoisie.

In spite of the differences between the Communists and Anarchists on other points both Communists and Anarchists accept this fundamental premise of class war. On the Red side you find powerful parties who advocate the extermination of a class as an essential means to an essential end. On the Nationalist side, no individual, whatever his class, is in danger unless proved guilty of crime, and any individual, whatever his class, is liable to be executed if he is charged and convicted of certain offences.

Secondly there is the question of scale. The correspondent of the *Manchester Guardian,* whose sympathies are strongly with the Left, asserts that the number of those executed in Madrid alone cannot be much less than 40,000. Sir Arthur Bryant who, as an historian, is accustomed to weigh evidence; has compared the estimates formed by correspondents in Madrid, Barcelona, Valencia and other cities, and examined a number of documents bearing on this point, believes that at least 350,000 men, women and children, have been murdered in Red Spain.

It is interesting to compare these estimates with the estimates of executions by the Spanish Inquisition. Lea, the Protestant historian of the Inquisition, accuses Llorente, a bitter enemy of the Inquisition, of gross exaggeration in his estimates, but let us accept Llorente's estimates for the purpose of comparison. His "extravagant guesses," to quote Lea, give 31,912 as the number of victims executed by the Inquisition from its foundation in 1480 up to 1808, a total of 328 years. Fewer people were executed by the Inquisition in the whole of Spain during three centuries than were murdered in Madrid in the first three months of the war.

14 THE PRISONER WHO PLEADED GUILTY

"ONE DOESN'T know what to believe. Each side accuses the other of atrocities."

Yes, and criminals frequently accuse the police of rough treatment.

One *does* know what to believe, for the criminal who pleads guilty in the face of overwhelming evidence is seldom acquitted by the jury, and by the Reds' own admission their guilt is removed from the realm of opinion to the realm of fact.

The Nationalist Government in Burgos published in October 1936 a preliminary official report on the atrocities committed by the Reds. The Spanish Embassy in London issued a reply. The Embassy "has not denied nor denies now that there have been excesses in the repressive conduct of the Government forces." The Embassy adds, "The Spanish Embassy in London does not, in fine, contradict the rebel pamphlet."

The *New Stateman* of November 14, 1936, says: "I am not on the strength of this going to deny that many and atrocious things have been done on the Government side;

they themselves with regret admitted as much, and so, for all I know, the greater part of the events described in this report are true."

The Red atrocities are therefore an accepted fact. The "Rebel Pamphlet" accepted as true by the Spanish Embassy deserves examination.

The facts and photographs in the Burgos Report are not contradicted by the Spanish Embassy. What is the story told by these facts and these photographs? First, that the Reds are not content to kill, but that in many cases they take a sadistic delight in torture. The obscene ingenuity of certain tortures is clearly pathological. Among the more horrifying exhibits in this Report is a photograph of the charred corpses of persons burned alive at Talavera.

The second fact that emerges is that these atrocities were inflicted not only on the rich but on the poor. Talavera, where I spent three days, is a small town mainly inhabited by poor people. The Burgos Report includes a poignant photograph of the bodies of seventeen proletarians who were murdered and thrown out into one of the streets of Talavera.

The first Burgos Report gives the names of eight paupers living in an old people's home, whose ages varied from 62 to 87. They were all killed with axes.

I conclude this chapter with a series of characteristic extracts from that first Burgos Report not contradicted by the Spanish Embassy. I quote nothing from the second and subsequent reports. My case against the Reds, I cannot too strongly insist, is based partly on the testimony of witnesses who may be presumed to be or to have been friendly to the Reds, and partly on the Burgos Report.

> On Wednesday, July 22nd, the day the Nationalist troops entered Arahal, the revolutionaries, seeing that their position was hopeless in face of the oncoming troops, perpetrated a crime arousing widespread indignation throughout Spain. They

despatched a band of desperados to the building where they had confined their prisoners, and, throwing buckets of petrol through the windows, set fire to it. Twenty-three people were burnt alive, and only one, Father Antonio Ramos, managed to escape, though badly burnt about the face and hands. The revolutionaries then fled, taking the keys of the prison with them to prevent the oncoming relief from rendering immediate aid to their victims. The Nationalist soldiers and Civil Guards who came to the rescue had to break down the doors with axes and picks.

On August 16th, at three o'clock, the Communist murderers began to throw hand grenades at the door of the school in order to terrify the prisoners and in the hope that, by a natural impulse to save themselves from the bombs, they would be driven into the very small courtyard at the back of the building. This was, in fact, what happened. As they ran out, a section of the revolutionaries' riflemen, stationed on the roofs of the adjoining houses, fired upon them. The wretched and terrified victims, faced on the one side with the intense bombardment from the street, and on the other with the hail of bullets when they entered the courtyard, were all thus exterminated in agony and confusion.

One man, whose name is not known, but who is alleged to have been a Fascist, was tied to an armoured car belonging to the revolutionaries, who dragged him through the streets, castrated him, and finally burnt him.

A peculiarly futile and senseless atrocity occurred when, in the full flush of their triumph, the revolutionaries decided to shoot every man in the place who, since the establishment of the republic in Spain, had been married in church by a priest. This was carried out even though among the advocates of this revolting futility were many who had been canonically married themselves.

The revolutionaries, discovering that the Nationalist trooops were approaching, resolved to butcher their prisoners. A woman called Concepción Velarde Caraballo, alias "La Caraballa," was first to urge the men to burn the gaol, and herself carried up the petrol. The prisoners were rounded-up in the small courtyard of the gaol and shot down, and, when all had fallen dead or wounded, their bodies were soaked with petrol and burnt, some of them while still alive.

When the Civil Guards arrived with the entry of the Nationalist troops, they actually witnessed several victims still writhing in the flames.

Ten persons were murdered, six of them burnt alive. Twenty buildings were also deliberately set on fire. . . . On the eve of the entry of the Nationalist troops into Campillo, the revolutionaries set about destroying the prison by raining bombs on it while it was being fired. To make sure that their victims should not excape, they also opened the prison doors and kept up a continuous rifle fusillade on any persons attempting to get out that way. In the end all the prisoners were either killed or wounded among the flames, but the executioners, noticing that there was a little life left in Dalmacio del Aguila Aguilar, and in Rafael López, killed off the former with dagger-thrusts and the latter by placing two bombs between his thighs and exploding them.

Many families had all their menfolk rounded up, and in most cases they were killed after revolting tortures. Cartloads of these wretched victims were taken at dawn to the cemetery, where they were made to dig a huge grave. Then the murderers fired on them, but they were careful to shoot them in the legs, so that they were not killed outright but fell writhing into the grave. Some were then buried alive and others left to linger in agony on the ground, where their cries and groans made the days and nights hideous, as they slowly died. The people living in the immediate neighbourhood, threatened with death themselves if they went to the aid of these unfortunate creatures, fled from their homes rather than endure these ghastly sights and sounds. Many of them have provided irrefutable evidence of these horrors, evidence grimly confirmed by the subsequent discovery of bodies with clenched hands protruding from the earth, and other cases where the wounded man had, by a supreme effort, managed to get his head above ground, and then could do no more.

When the revolutionaries committed these murders, they always took with them two prisoners from among those remaining in the prison, as witnesses. These latter were then sent back to the prison with promises that their lives would be spared, thus arousing false hopes. In many cases, where entire families were in prison, the usual procedure was to shoot one member of the family each day, starting with the sons and finishing with the father, in order to give the maximum of mental anguish in addition to physical torture.

Of the twenty-eight Civil Guards, only eight have survived. They pierced the eyes of one of them, Agustín Menacho, with a needle, and then shot him. The total number of anti-Communists and Civil Guards killed in Lora del Rio was 138.

These facts have been gathered from the statements of a number of responsible witnesses who were present at the events described. Among them is the magistrate of Lora del Río, Don Eugenio Pico Martín, who was arrested during the first few days of the revolutionary occupation, but was later set free on condition that he reported daily to the Soviet. Another is one of the surviving Civil Guards of Lora, Cristóbal Calvante Granados. A third is Don José María Linán, local leader of the Spanish Phalanx. He was taken prisoner from the beginning of the upheaval and was to have been shot on the night of the day when the Nationalist troops arrived to liberate the village.

Doña Blanca de Lucía, a widow of sixty-two, a chemist, was murdered in peculiarly revolting circumstances. A number of men burst into her house, accompanied by one woman. The latter stripped Doña Blanca, who was at once outraged by one of the ruffians. They then allowed her to dress on condition that she went away at once to Penaflor on foot. As she made to leave the house they shot and severely wounded her. They then tied a heavy stone round her neck, dragged her to the river and threw her in.

The remaining victims were murdered by means of the procedure butchers called "the little walk." This consisted in walking them through the streets to be subjected to the most abject humiliations on the part of the revolutionary rabble and then having them shot dead by lads from 16 to 18 years of age.

The family of Don Cristóbal Romero Martel, well known in the village for their piety and charity, were besieged in their own house for five days by the Communist rabble. Because of their high religious principles, and because they could not bring themselves to believe that the mob would really murder them after all the help and kindness received at the hands of the family in the past, this gentleman and his two sons, although armed, refrained from killing any of their besiegers and confined themselves to passive resistance. On the fourth day of the siege, the incendiary bombs of the attackers set fire to the house, while a band of ruffians broke down the doors and began to loot and destroy the place. Señor Romero, with his wife, his two sons, and their fiancées, then fled to the roof of the house, but their adversaries followed, and two men of the party were cruelly murdered in spite of the tears and prayers of the women, who vainly tried to shelter them in their arms. The ladies, by a miracle, escaped unharmed, except the mother, who had bullet wounds in the face. Old Don Cristóbal, with a fractured skull and one eye half out of its socket, still remained alive, but the murderers were insatiable. They fell upon him with axes, encouraging a boy of twelve to rain blows upon the dying man, who finally expired asking pardon for his murderers.

15 THE CHARGES AGAINST THE NATIONALIST TROOPS

No PROFOUND knowledge of human nature would have been necessary to foresee the practice the Valencia Government would adopt once they realized the futility of denying that appalling atrocities had been committed in Red Spain. The only hope of distracting attention from their crimes was to fabricate mythical atrocities. Such tactics had every chance of success in England, for they appeal to our British love of a compromise, and they flatter our national vanity. It is pleasant to believe that Englishmen are divided not only from Spanish Communists, but from Spaniards as a whole by a moral gulf.

Those who have not the leisure to examine the evidence should withhold judgment. They should not accuse either side of atrocities unless they are prepared to support this accusation with facts. Nobody is obliged to express an opinion on the charges and counter-charges of atrocities, but it is unfair to brand all Spaniards indiscriminately as guilty of odious crimes merely because one cannot be bothered to examine the available evidence.

The most popular of all Red myths is the famous

massacre at Badajoz. This is not the historical massacre by Wellington's troops in the Peninsula War, but the fictitious massacre by the Nationalists. This myth was exposed in *Time*, an American news-weekly by no means friendly to Franco:

"The day of the capture of Badajoz" (by the Whites), declared World Trend Features, "the figure of two thousand Reds shot was given by the French Havas correspondent who was not there but in Portugal. All over the world this figure was taken up and printed. Next day John Elliott, of the *New York Herald Tribune*, was the first American correspondent, and probably the first non-Spanish correspondent, to enter Badajoz. He saw no signs of the shootings, so didn't report them. He was promptly condemned by some of his own *Herald Tribune* colleagues for 'having sold out to the Fascists.' Each of the great international Press Services is faking in its Paris bureau, and each says it has to do so to keep up with the 'colourful competition' of the others."

I have already quoted from *Three Pictures of the Spanish War*, in which a Liberal under the pseudonym of "Don Justo Medio" sums up, after the opposing views of the Whites and the Reds have been stated:

> About nothing have wilder statements been made than about the mass executions carried out by the insurgents. I have compared, for example, all available accounts in Spanish, French or English, eleven in number, of the alleged mass of executions at Badajoz in August, 1936. The total number of persons alleged to have been executed varies from 400 to 2,500; the contradictory accounts of the executions fall into three well-marked groups; two different places were given where the executions are supposed to have been perpetrated; while several accounts, deficient also in other essential details, give no place at all.

The death blow to the Badajoz legend is provided by

Major Geoffrey McNeill-Moss in his fine book, *The Epic of the Alcázar*. This massacre was reported in the *New York Herald Tribune*, under the signature of Reynolds Packard, who was never in Badajoz, and was in Portugal at the time the mythical massacre was reported. His story was telegraphed all over the world. He has since protested vigorously against the misuse of his name, attached to a fake report written by the Reds. "The official correspondents of the Havas Agency," to whom similar telegrams were attributed, "seem to have had somewhat the same sort of trouble as Mr. Packard." For a detailed analysis of their reports and disclaimers see *The Epic of the Alcázar*.

Second only in popularity to the myth of Badajoz is the legend of Guernica. Here is Douglas Jerrold's analysis of the Guernica story:

> Firstly, Guernica is a strategic position of considerable importance. Secondly, it is the centre of an important part of the Basque small-arms industry. Thirdly, by the official admission of the Mayor, in his statement issued by the Bilbao Government and communicated to the Press all over the world, Guernica was full of troops when it was bombed. Fourthly, Guernica was bombed in the proper course of the operations against Bilbao, but it was not bombed on the day that it was burnt, and it was burnt by the retreating Basque (or, more probably, by the Asturian) troops, and not by the Nationalist forces.
>
> Let us examine the evidence for these statements.
>
> No evidence is required for the first two. The strategic importance of Guernica is obvious to any soldier who looks at the map. That it is surrounded by small-arms factories is also a matter of established fact. The owners of these factories, incidentally, have for years been supplying arms to terrorists and other illegal organizations all over Europe and Asia. But what of the Dean of Valladolid, who was in the town when it was burnt; of *The Times* correspondent, who saw the aeroplanes *en route:* of the two German airmen, whose diaries with military conciseness contained the simple word "Guernica" against the required date?

As regards the Dean of Valladolid, the ecclesiastical authorities in Valladolid say that the priest in question is not the Dean. Nor is the case for his veracity improved by the discovery that he is the author of another account of the bombardment appearing under another signature, and confirming that which appeared under his own name. *The Times* correspondent was in Bilbao when, like everyone else there, he heard accounts of Guernica. He went to Guernica in the small hours of the following morning. His first excited account began with the statement that the town was completely destroyed, but that the deaths were, fortunately, small. They could hardly have been small if the town had been slowly, systematically, pounded to pieces. They might have been if it was being fired and mined. He was eight and a half miles away from Guernica when he "saw" the aeroplanes, and he was certainly in Bilbao when he wrote his despatch. As to the Germans, we have no right whatever to accept the reports of their evidence, but there is no reason to doubt that they bombed Guernica on occasions. It had been bombed intermittently for several days before it was given up.

On the other side, the evidence is, as near as may be, conclusive. The correspondents of the Havas agency, of *The Times*, and of several other newspapers have affirmed positively that most of the damage which they saw was wrought not by bombing, but by deliberate destruction by fires from the ground. The statements are explicit. There were only a few bomb holes, and the walls of the houses in the quarter most completely destroyed bear no marks of bomb splinters. Nor can the damage done by a bomb and that done by dynamiters and incendiaries be confused by any competent observer.

And yet, without this testimony from *The Times* correspondent and other neutral journalists, I should feel justified in denying the charge of wanton destruction for quite different reasons. Firstly, I have seen the destruction at Irún, which was admittedly wrought by the same army, under the same leadership, as that which was defending Guernica: a complete street—the principal street of the town—systematically destroyed, house by house, with only the walls left standing, and the interiors completely gutted by fire. A rain of bombs might, in loose journalistic parlance, "destroy" a whole street in a town, but it would not destroy it *in that way*. At Guernica, as at Irún, there is hardly a mark in the street. A "rain of bombs" would fall as often in the streets and gardens as on the houses, and must leave traces which could not possibly be obliterated. The roadway would be destroyed, the flowers would be withered. Secondly, people who talk about destruction from the air have no idea of the local effect of a bomb. I have seen, at Málaga and elsewhere, the effect of bombs on a score of houses. A bomb falling from a height will tear its way through a house and explode, leaving half the house standing. That part of the house which it hits, however, will be totally destroyed; the burst will be outwards as well as upwards, and the outside walls will never be left intact. To destroy an entire small town, however, as part of Irún was destroyed, not hundreds, but thousands, of bombs would be required. The resources for such wholesale destruction are entirely lacking to either side in this war. Apart altogether from the question of expediency, such destruction would mean using a month's supply of ammunition for General Franco's entire army, and denuding all fronts of air protection to indulge in an orgy of lunatic folly.

And again, Eibar was also, and admittedly, burnt. It was never suggested by Bilbao that it had even been severely bombed till two days after the Guernica story had shocked the world. Yet eye-witnesses report that the damage at Eibar is of precisely the same kind as that at Guernica.

Finally, the question can be cynically determined by reference to that old question "*cui bono?*" When the alleged destruction of Guernica took place it was in process of being evacuated; an advance had taken place on all fronts, and nothing could have saved the town. General Franco had nothing whatever to gain by destroying it. The Basque Government, if they could get their story accepted, had everything to gain. The "incident" would stiffen the resistance of the Catholic Basques. It would influence neutral opinion, strengthen the attitude of the British Government in regard to the blockade of Bilbao, and possibly even lead to its abandonment.

A distinguished and senior officer in the Air Force tells

me that it is impossible in modern war to draw any ethical distinction between one kind of target and another. Every town contains citizens who are contributing to the conduct of the war either by making munitions or by contributing to the essential supplies. He tells me that professional airmen are mildly contemptuous of the nonsense talked by civilians on this subject. In the next war we shall probably begin by attempting to destroy the enemy's aerodromes, but we shall certainly not refrain from bombing his towns if there is any advantage to be gained thereby.

I visited Avila and Talavera, open towns, shortly after they were bombarded, and I was in Málaga, where no troops were visible, within a few hours of Málaga's being shelled from the sea. I should have felt no particular grievance against the Reds had I been bombed from the air.

A Red defeat is always accompanied by a spate of atrocity stories, and the fall of Madrid probably will prove to be no exception. The Reds will have broadcast their myths almost before the city surrenders. Some popularity-seeking cleric will scold Franco from the pulpit and in the Press, and a week or two later the true account of what has happened will be issued from Salamanca and published in small print on a back page.

If we ignore the statements of the witnesses hostile to Franco, very little remains of the case against the Nationalist troops. So far as I know, the only writer who is friendly to Franco, might be subpœnaed by the Reds for the prosecution, is Helen Nicholson, whose book, *Death in the Morning,* has already been referred to. Her book describes Granada during the siege.

The surrounding country was dominated by the Reds, and Granada was held by a minute garrison, whose position was compromised by such hostile elements as remained in the town. Men who are holding out against great odds seldom show mercy to the enemy within the gates, and Granada was no exception to this general rule. Spy fever was no doubt as rampant in Granada as in Great Britain during the Great War, and no mercy was shown either to Communists or Anarchists or to those who harboured the declared enemies of Nationalist Spain. You have only to read the chapter on Málaga in Sir Peter Chalmers-Mitchell's book to realise why no mercy could be expected by such active members of Communist and Anarchist organisations as fell into the hands of the Nationalists.

Sir Peter, whose sympathies are with the extreme Left, describes the incessant murders committed by these men. It is not surprising that some Communists and Anarchists have been shot; it is surprising that so *few* have been shot.

Helen Nicholson saw two men and a Communist they had sheltered in defiance of the regulations driven off in a lorry; she was told that they were being driven to execution. The men had been beaten by the Fascists to make them confess.

> The summary executions that filled everyone with disgust and horror were recognized, with some reluctance, as a war-time measure which must be endured. Whatever errors or harshnesses were committed by the military authorities, they were as milk-and-water compared to the calculated brutalities of the Reds.

Left-Wing reviewers have dismissed as "mere hearsay" Helen Nicholson's account of Red atrocities, and accepted as direct evidence her testimony as to the execution of Communists in Granada. I do wish people would use technical terms in their correct sense. Helen Nicholson *witnessed* no executions, though she saw prisoners, who had been beaten to make them confess, being driven off, *presumably* to execution, and her evidence of atrocities, on both sides, is mostly, but not entirely, hearsay evidence:

> At the taking of Almendralejo they [the Moorish troops] wept like children at the sight of the prison courtyard where the Reds had crucified the prisoners around the walls. These were

political hostages taken from Catholic families. The bodies still hung there, with their feet and legs burned away—petrol had been poured over them and set alight, while the victims were still living.

This is not hearsay evidence, for the Portuguese journalist Feliz Corrlia *witnessed* this scene, and had sworn an affidavit to this effect. The important distinction is that between witnesses friendly and unfriendly to those who are charged with atrocities. Helen Nicholson, as the mother of a Spanish Nationalist, is an impressive witness against the Nationalists, whereas the Portuguese journalist is less impressive as a witness against the Reds, as most Portuguese are hostile to the Reds. Moreover, I have checked the Portuguese account with the second Burgos report on atrocities and suspect his story of exaggeration.

"The prisoners in the convent," I am quoting from the official report, "crowded into the church, and on hearing the first shot of the liberating army, the Communists began to sling bombs and bottles containing inflammable liquids at their victims. These horrors lasted until five in the afternoon, and those who had escaped death were set free by the Nationalist troops."

A detailed list of those who were killed, wounded and burned is given in the report.

The contrast between the Portuguese statement and the official report confirms the integrity of those who prepared this report, and the sincerity of their ambition to confine themselves to facts proved beyond all possible doubt.

Though many stories of Red atrocities heard by Mrs. Nicholson are probably true, my case against the Reds would be weakened if I quoted statements for which no adequate evidence is offered in her book. I have no wish to emulate the methods adopted in compiling the atrocity reports issued by the Spanish Embassy in London. On the other hand, I am impressed by her story of firsthand interviews with victims of the Reds. I know from my own experience in Spain that there is a world of difference between the way Spaniards retail hearsay atrocities, and the way people describe what has happened to themselves. I do not claim any special intuition, but the look in the eyes of a man who has *seen* such things is unmistakable. In the discussion of atrocities I have limited myself to evidence as evidence is understood in a court of law, and the expression of remembered evil one sees on the faces of those who have suffered is not evidence, nor can those who have seen this expression translate it into words or pass on to the reader his sense of certainty. But to one who has been in wartime Spain there is a ring of truth in the record of the author's meeting with a lady in Seville.

> She spoke in a low voice, very quietly: "I have seen terrible sights—babies less than a year old, with knives thrust through their little bodies. . . . Men whose arms had been cut off. I hope," she went on in the same monotonous, unemotional tone, "that some of the mutilated ones will live, so that people can see them, and know what the Communists have done. People can't believe such things, you know, unless they've seen them."

And that, alas, is the difficulty. One cannot say, "Blessed are those who have not seen and yet have believed." Not blessed, only intelligent.

16 "THE SAD AND BITTER PROFILE"

LET US SUPPOSE that a Popular Front came into power in Great Britain, and that their supporters during the election campaign included leading Liberals such as Professor Gilbert Murray and Mr. H.A.L. Fisher, and eminent scientists with Left-Wing sympathies such as Sir Peter Chalmers-Mitchell and Professor J.B.S. Haldane, and let us suppose that during the first session of the new Parliament St. Paul's cathedral and the office of *The Times* were burned to the ground, and that the police and the fire brigade had instructions from the Government not to interfere. Let us assume that leading Conservatives were murdered by the score, that their murderers were not brought to justice, and that as a culmination to these atrocities Mr. Neville Chamberlain, the Leader of the Opposition, was assassinated by four policemen acting under the instructions of Scotland Yard.

To make our analogy complete we must further assume that Professor Gilbert Murray, Mr. H.A.L. Fisher, Professor Haldane and Sir Peter Chalmers-Mitchell fled to Italy and published statements in which they expressed their great regret for the part they had played in bringing the Popular Front into power.

Leading Liberals such as Madariaga, Unamuno and Lerroux, idolized by Bloomsbury intellectuals while they were regarded as supporters of the Left, differ from English Liberals in two important respects. They know Spain and they do not support the Valencia Government.

It has been suggested that Unamuno, the famous Rector of Salamanca, wavered in his support of the Nationalist cause. Nobody, however, has claimed that he transferred his allegiance to the Red Government. He is said to have made an impatient comment on the presence of the Italians in Salamanca. Similar comments were often heard on the lips of Frenchmen during the Great War, but even those Frenchmen who most bitterly resented the friendly invasion of Paris by officers on leave from the British and American armies, were never suspected of waning devotion to the national cause.

In Spain, as in Russia and in revolutionary France, the intellectuals who preached revolution have lived to regret the results of their crusade.

"This is not it," exclaimed José Ortega y Gasset, deputy and Professor at the University of Madrid, "this is not it; the Republic has a sad and bitter profile."

Eduardo Ortega y Gasset, the leader of the Radical Socialist Left, was no less disillusioned. "The Republic fails by the incompetence, laziness and vanity of its rulers, who strive to disguise their incapacity behind a series of exceptional measures that outrage the spirit of democracy essential to the régime."

Señor García Valdecasas, Professor at the University of Granada, wrote: "Those who failed as rulers have been succeeded by men, already devoid of prestige, who are incapable of understanding the august function of leadership, and who rival each other in the task of destruction. . . . Spain is being impoverished. Consternation will spread when the country learns the value of the cattle that have been destroyed, the trees that have been cut down, the setback suffered by agriculture, the paralysation of credit, and the general annihilation of wealth."

Nobody would have deduced from our Left-Wing Press that the sun of Republicanism had risen on so sad a scene, but the lawlessness in the early years of the Republic was only the prelude to the Red Terror following the election of the "Popular Front." This Red Terror drove Radicals like Lerroux, the doyen of Spanish Republicans, and more than once Premier in Republican Spain, into the Nationalist camp.

Radicals in our own country who are flirting with Communism should be warned by the fate, when the war broke out, of Radicals in Valencia.

"There are many," wrote Lerroux, "of whom nothing has been heard and of whom one fears to have tidings. In the city and province of Valencia not only the Radical Deputies have been murdered, but in certain villages all members of the Radical Party have been exterminated. At Málaga and Alicante the Radicals were literally hunted down. The blood toll taken of the Radical Party in Spain is far greater than that taken of the Church and, perhaps, than that taken of the Civil Guard, so savagely sacrificed."

Alcalá Zamora, President when the Popular Front came into power, described how easily the extremists terrorized the weak and vacillating Moderates. "The Government allowed the mob, by now fallen prey to the agitators, to become masters of the streets and of the Government itself."

Don Salvador de Madariaga is the author of an excellent book on Spain. His attitude to the Reds might be described as one of malevolent neutrality. He does not support Franco, but no Nationalist has been more caustic in his comments on our Left-Wing intellectuals.

> Led by a kind of mental inertia [he writes] to take for granted that all that lies on the left is liberal, many of these men have

overlooked the tremendous significance of the abjuration by the masses of that Liberalism to which they owe their emancipation. The intellectual sympathizers with Communism have not been deterred by the explicit contempt for Liberalism in general, and for liberty of thought in particular, which is one of the few features of Communism to be found both in its theory and in its practice. They do not seem to be in the least perturbed by the obvious subversion of values implied in the deliberate humiliation of the mental worker considered by Communism as the auxiliary of the manual worker; and even now, after so much experience, they go on cheerfully confusing the issue not only between Communism and democracy, which is bad enough, but between Communism and liberty, which would be comic if it were not tragic.

We are asked to believe that the issue is between Fascism and Communism, and, in the name of democracy and liberty, we are bidden to espouse the cause of Communism.

The most striking condemnation of the Popular Front is the *mea culpa* of Dr. Gregorio Marañón. Marañón is the President of the Academy of Medicine of Madrid and famous for his discoveries in connection with the endocrine glands. His book, *Problem of the Sexes,* has been translated into nearly every language. He was a deputy in the Cortes and one of the founders of the Republic. He is a Radical who has proved his convictions by suffering for them. He was imprisoned under the dictator Primo de Rivera at a time when Largo Caballero was drawing handsome pay as a Councillor of State, and this is what he says:

> My true story? It is an act of contrition!
> I have been misled, I have been mistaken. Save for a few new-fangled Catholics who persist in their prejudice in favour of the Communists, all the intellectuals of Spain think as I do, speak as I do, and, like me, have had to flee from Republican Spain to save their lives.
> From the standpoint of a scientist one should recognize one's mistakes.

Peccavi! The Revolution was brought about by us. We desired it and prepared it; and it sprang from our strongest reactions against the outrages which freedom of thought suffered. The execution of Ferrer[1] produced a feeling of revulsion in me. The Monarchy dealt itself a death blow by killing Ferrer. From the blood of another martyr, the journalist Sirval,[2] who was killed in prison during the Asturian affair, the Popular Front was two years later to draw its strength in propaganda.

True, our intellectual standing had already stamped us as the representatives of progress over against the old historic Spain, but Ferrer and Sirval furnished the decisive sentimental argument that inflamed us.

But what has happened since then? You know what has happened; but I have seen it. Thirty thousand Ferrers, guilty of freedom of thought, have been shot without a trial. Five thousand Sirvals have been killed in prison with hand-grenades.

Thousands of men and women are still being murdered every day on the mere suspicion of independence of opinion.

The same acts have led to the same reactions on my part. I did not wait for these hecatombs to dissociate myself from stupid murderers, from frenzied primitives, who hate all science and intellect. . . .

The present situation allows of no half-way house. . . . Franco is certain to win, and his victory will give me the greatest satisfaction. In any case, there can be no comparison between the two régimes. Primo de Rivera's dictatorship, from which I suffered personally and bodily, was, compared with the Red tyranny, an amiable dictatorship. The intellectuals

---

[1] Francisco Ferrer, radical educator who conducted his school in Barcelona in accordance with Tolstoyan principles and those of the celebrated A.S. Neill of Summerhill, executed in 1909 following disorders with which he had no connection.

[2] Luis Sirval, journalist, arrested and murdered in prison by Nationalist officers after he published protests against Nationalist reprisals against the defeated miners of Asturias in 1934.

who were fortunate enough to be residing in the territory under Nationalist control have neither had their lives threatened nor been obliged to go into exile.

You can see for yourself. In all the hotels in Paris and in the large towns of France you will find political refugees from Spain. All of them are people who have escaped from Red Spain. Not one has found it necessary to leave Nationalist Spain.

Only one thing matters: that Spain, Europe, and mankind should be freed from a system of bloodshed, an institution of murder, which we accuse ourselves of having incurred while labouring under a tragic misapprehension.

POSTSCRIPT: AFTERTHOUGHTS ON THE SPANISH WAR*

I NEED NOT REPEAT in this chapter the reasons given in my book *Spanish Rehearsal* for believing in the justice of General Franco's cause, nor my experiences, described in that book, during my first journey through Spain at war. The war and the controversy which it provoked have both come to an end, but to those who are still interested in the background of the Spanish struggle I commend one of the most interesting autobiographies of our day, Douglas Jerrold's *Georgian Adventure*. It was Jerrold who made the arrangements for the aeroplane that carried three British tourists to the Balearic Islands, and left (without the tourists) with General Franco for Morocco on the day before the rising began.

Franco's final victory was rendered possible by two decisive battles:—the first united the armies of Franco and Mola in 1936; the second, in 1938, separated the defenders of Barcelona from the defenders of Madrid.

*These excerpts are from my Autobiography, *Come What May*, published in 1941.

I returned to Spain at the beginning of April, 1938, and saw the final phases of the battle for the sea.

On arriving at Saragossa I met an officer who greeted me with the words, "To-day our outposts saw the sea." He said these words with a mystical enthusiasm I shall never forget.

Thalassa! Thalassa! But the sea meant more to those who had to fight every yard of their advance than it could have meant to Xenophon's army.

On Wednesday, April 13, we returned to Morella. We left our cars within a few yards of a battery of big guns. Other batteries were in action half a mile down the road. The violence of their dispute echoed from the mountain walls. Their immediate objective was the Republican artillery which had been shelling our road in an attempt to locate our batteries. A noise of angry wings above and a flight of thirty bombers swept across the sky to administer the *coup de grâce* to the Republican artillery.

The Republican anti-aircraft spluttered an indignant protest, and the blue heaven was flaked with white cloudlets; the eagles of Spain dived disdainfully through them. The hills re-echoed to the continuous thunder of their bombs.

I was to pass the Easter week-end with three friends of mine who took part in this attack. I knew that they were at the front. The planes dived perilously near the artillery, and returned unscathed across the lines. An hour later they were back again.

We left our cars and started up the hillside towards an artillery observation post above the valley. Many a time I have scrambled in a crescendo of excitement up the last yards leading to an Alpine pass, but never with a greater sense of expectancy than on the final slope of this nameless hill. I broke into a run on the last incline of limestone boulders, and suddenly the ground fell away from my feet. Beyond the plain and the ultimate hills was a thin blue strip—*Thalassa! Thalassa!*

The artillery observation officer spoke fluent English. He was sixteen when war broke out, and spent the first six months of the war in London. This was not the first day outposts had seen the sea, but it was the first day artillery observation posts commanded the Mediterranean.

"To-day for the first time," said the boy, "I saw the sea." *For the first time.* I knew what he meant. I, too, felt as if I had never really seen the sea until I saw it from this Spanish hill.

The battle was dying down. Through glasses we could see the Nationalists occupying a ridge; the Republicans had retreated, and a long line of tanks were going into action against a burning village, whose outskirts were still defended by the enemy. A Russian tank—we photographed it next day—had just been put out of action in a road the Nationalists had not yet occupied. Another tank could be seen cautiously moving up the road towards its disabled companion. A few shells burst; the rescuing tank hesitated, paused, turned tail and fled.

We spent three lazy hours watching the dying battle. The air was fragrant with spring and the ground where we lay was graced by April flowers. The soft outlines of these southern hills melting into a blue mist, the Mediterranean, recalled indolent hours among the mountains of peace. The war seemed curiously unreal. Even the sights and sounds of battle seemed to translate themselves naturally into mountain terms—the white puffs of bursting shells into clouds, the thunder of distant avalanches. But the war broke through this mountain reverie when the Republican planes came over.

"Red aeroplanes," said the artillery officer; "we know they're Red because we can't see them."

This was true enough, for though we could hear the aeroplanes as they swept over us, they were flying so high they were invisible. They must have been flying at a height of over 20,000 feet. "Their best fighters have been killed," he continued, "and the pilots who have now replaced them are not properly trained and their morale is bad. That's why they fly so high."

We regained our cars as the sun set, and on our return journey we met lorry after lorry bringing the troops that were to fight next day. A vivid memory of a memorable day is the silhouette of a lorry full of sombre, hooded Moors seen against the last glow of the evening sky.

Morella, where we slept, is a small town with one hotel commandeered for the General. We arrived at nine, and at eleven our Press officer returned with the good news that the Mayor had placed at our disposal three beds in a private house, beds vacated by cavalry officers who had left that afternoon for the front. Their soldier servants had remained behind, and refused to permit us to occupy the beds allotted to us by the obliging Mayor. So the Press officer went off in search of a military patrol, while we paced up and down outside the gates of a somewhat dingy paradise. Along the distant mountain line the camp-fires were burning, and the lowering clouds inspired a proper feeling of gratitude for the prospect, however dubious, of a shelter, however poor.

The Press officer returned with a corporal and two military policemen. The faithful servants of the departed cavalry officers surrendered the fort at discretion, and we marched in and took possession of three beds for four people. There was a fourth bed, but it had no mattress, for the Republicans had removed most of the mattresses and every available blanket from Morella. It was excessively cold, and my companions did not sleep until dawn. I was more fortunate, and woke thoroughly refreshed. The threatening storm had passed, and the sky was cloudless. I paid a short visit to the beautiful little church, which had miraculously escaped destruction, as had its priest, who spent eighteen months in a mountain cave with the Mayor of Morella. As I came out of the church I saw a flight of bombers pass over the town on their way to the last defences of the Republicans in this battle for the sea.

Few experiences are more exhilarating than to follow the day-by-day advance of a victorious army. We drove rapidly down the road to the sea, left behind us the ridge which had been captured from the Republicans when I first visited this front, drove through a village the Republicans had been driven from on the previous day, and emerged in a pleasant little valley on to open ground where only one low-lying ridge still separated us from the redemption of the sea. We turned a corner to find the artillery in action. The batteries were firing from a point just behind an abrupt ridge; from the summit we watched the battle for the last and lowest of the hill barriers separating the Nationalists from the low ground leading to the sea. Through our glasses we could just see the reserves moving up to the slopes where the front line had been established. We could follow every phase of the offensive. The preliminary bombardment had already been in progress for more than an hour, and the big shells were still bursting beyond the ridge, hurling vast sulphurous clouds into the sky. Then followed the shrapnel barrage, which burst, not on the ground, but in the sky, so that the ridge was rimmed with thunder clouds. A pause and the hills re-echoed to the vicious splutter of machine-guns punctured by the staccato of hand grenade and bomb, as the infantry advanced to storm the front lines. The duel between machine-gun and grenade lasted for about twenty minutes, and then suddenly the clamour faded into silence. Had the attack succeeded or failed?

"We shall soon know," said the Press officer. "If the attack has failed the bombardment will begin again."

We rejoined the car and drove down the road leading to the ridge which had just been captured, and entered Chert three hours after the village had been captured by the Nationalists. Three tanks had halted in the main square, for a Russian tank was round the corner. "They've sent for an anti-tank gun," said the Press officer, "to put the Russian out of his misery."

A woman came out of a house and blinked timidly. And

then she smiled. It was true, it was really true. The Republicans had gone. The nightmare had passed. There were the soldiers making a bonfire of those monotonous Republican posters—"*No paserán*" going up in flames. A group of villagers gathered round our Press officer and overwhelmed him in a flood of cheerful babble. A girl just on the edge of this group kept on chanting a kind of lyrical refrain: "They said '*No paserán*,' but they have passed [chuckle]. They said '*No paserán*,' but they *did* pass [more chuckles]."

An old lady explained that she had not tasted bread for a month, but she had managed to get a piece of meat and had hidden it very carefully. But not carefully enough. That morning the Republicans had come round on a last looting foray, and had found the meat. The Republican planes returned, and the anti-aircraft imprinted its pattern on the sky, and the old lady repeated her moan about the meat.

As we left Chert the Republicans started a counter-offensive on the ridge they had lost. We were near enough to see the infantry without glasses. I remember a group near the top of the ridge huddled against a stone wall as the shells exploded just below them. War in Spain retained something of the colourful pageantry of the Middle Ages. The infantry went into battle behind an immense banner planted in triumph at every stage of the advance, marking the frontier between the Spain that had been saved and the Spain still unredeemed. The colours of Nationalist Spain are the same as those of the M.C.C., and the familiar red and yellow glimpsed between the clouds of exploding shells awoke very different memories—idle hours at Lord's, M.C.C. flags drooping listlessly in the summer haze.

The bombardment ceased. We saw a wave of little figures stumbling across the skyline. Some fell. We went back to our car, and round the next corner met the anti-tank gun towed by a car at racing speed. We passed in rapid succession three lorries crowded with reinforcements, but the counter-attack was already dying down. The Republicans were irrational fighters, for it is unreasonable to abandon positions of great natural strength if you feel yourself strong enough to attempt their recapture within an hour of losing them. Forces which are not strong enough to hold can hardly be expected to recapture the crest of a mountain ridge.

Two days later the Nationalists reached the sea.

Our journey back to Morella was slow, for we were driving against the stream of traffic—infantry, cavalry, big guns, and a long procession of pack mules loaded with ammunition. *And there with the rest were the lads who would never be old.* I thought of Housman's lines as we passed lorry after lorry of young men, their faces turned towards the sea. Many of those we saw on those memorable days were destined to

> Carry back straight to the coiner the mintage of man,
> The lads that will die in their glory and never be old.

Barcelona made most of the shirts worn in Spain, a fact which might have been deduced from the appearance of the Nationalist army. Anything in the nature of a shirt was welcome, and no questions were asked. I saw one soldier with a loud check pattern protruding cheeringly through a sheepskin coat. A few officers in smart khaki set a tone which the troops made no attempt to maintain. They reminded me of old pictures of the Confederates during the last stages of the American Civil War. I liked the hats, ranging from a magnificent straw hat, which would have pleased a Mexican cowboy, to Carlists' berets. Nor was there any drab uniformity about the lorries, particularly those of the Moors. An incongruous effect was produced by the mascot of a large inane doll dangling just beneath a fierce Moor stretched out on the top of a van, the roof shared with a Mickey Mouse, a dead calf, a live hen and a mattress. For the Moor likes to lie soft if he can, even on the field of battle.

Halfway to Morella a German officer in the car ahead jumped out into the road, shouted *"Avions!"* and made for the field. "Get out," said the Press officer. So we got out. The bull's-eye is the safest part of a target when aeroplanes are flying at the height favoured by the Republicans, so I decided not to follow the Germans into the field, and before lying down in the ditch, to minimise the danger of flying fragments of anti-aircraft, I cautiously searched the heavens; for I was wearing the less disreputable of two disreputable suits, and hoped to see General Franco within a few days. I could neither see nor hear the aeroplanes; this was not surprising, for it had been a false alarm. I climbed back into the car, composing my own epitaph on the assumption that my reluctance to spoil my suiting had proved fatal:

> He died as he lived
> A martyr to Good Form
> Keeping up Appearances to the Last.

From the small pass we descended to Morella where two roads diverge, reuniting lower down. The authorities had naturally made these one-way roads. In the morning we met three lorries coming down the road for ascending cars, and it was nice to round off the day by dodging two lorries charging cheerfully up the road reserved for the descending traffic. Spaniards have no sense of motoring sin. A few days before our driver had passed a car on the bend of a mountain road and met a lorry which obligingly took to the ditch. In England our driver would have been the target for colourful abuse, and would have been properly contrite. But the lorry driver was not perturbed, and our driver was not penitent.

Night fell as we left Morella. The hills just beyond were full of Republican stragglers, who sometimes held up cars and sometimes strung a row of bombs across the road wind-screen high; but the trivial risk of such playful pranks was more than offset by the relief of seeing the lamps of the oncoming lorries before we met them round a bend. I confess to these fears with shame, and am consoled by the reflection that a Spanish general noted for his personal bravery remarked that the one thing in this war which really frightened him was the return from the front against the stream of unending lorries driven by light-hearted Spaniards.

It was on Easter Saturday that the Nationalists captured Viñaroz, on the Mediterranean. The Republican armies to the north and south were finally separated and the battle of the sea had been won. Never have I heard on the radio a voice more vibrant with emotion than the voice of the Nationalist broadcaster when he announced that the vanguard had reached the sea. Three pilots staying with the Infante grasped each other by the hand and gambolled round the room with delight. Much might yet pass before the final surrender, but the war had been won.

The effective choice in Spain was not between a Fascist dictatorship and parliamentary democracy, for Communism had destroyed democracy in Spain; but between a dictatorship under which Christianity could survive, and a dictatorship which had already eliminated organised religion from the territories under its control. The massacre of priests and the destruction of churches convinced Liberals and Protestants, such as my father, and thousands of Catholics who had no belief in dictatorships, whether of the Right or of the Left, and who would have readily endorsed the verdict of the great French historian, Alexis de Tocqueville, on the consequences of unlimited power, to rally for the support of General Franco.

"Unlimited power," wrote de Tocqueville, "appears to me to be in itself an evil, and a dangerous thing, and the mind of man unequal to the disinterested practice of omnipotence. I think that God alone can exercise supreme and uncontrolled power, because His wisdom and justice are eternally proportionate to His might. But no power on earth is so worthy of honour for itself, or of reverential obedience to the rights which it represents, that I would consent to admit its uncontrolled and all-predominant authority. When I see the right and the means of absolute command are conferred on a people or upon an aristocracy or a democracy, a monarchy or a republic, I recognise the germ of tyranny."

It is relevant to consider the reasons for the Republican defeat, for we may still profit by drawing correct deductions from their failure.

The Republicans began the war with almost everything in their favour. They were in possession of all the great centres of industry. The gold reserves were in their hands. The fleet had rallied to their side. The Nationalist risings in Madrid and in Barcelona had failed. Franco had to begin the reconquest of Spain from Morocco, across Straits in control of a hostile fleet.

On balance the Republicans received as much assistance from France and Russia as the Nationalists from Germany and Italy.

The Republicans lost because they sacrificed military to political considerations. The war was regarded as a means to an end, political revolution. Officers were appointed for political reasons. The army was "democratised," and the regular officers who remained loyal to the Republic were regarded with profound suspicion. Now there is no reason why officers, like priests, should not be recruited from every social stratum. But unless the officer, like the priest, feels himself to be the representative of a hierarchic tradition, set apart from other men, he will lack the confidence in himself and the power to impose respect essential in the ordeal of battle. Democratic formulas cannot be applied in war, which is in essence aristocratic, for leadership in war, to be effective, must be imposed from above, not dictated from below. There were many gallant officers in the Republican army, but there was no sense of hierarchic solidarity. Many a battalion surrendered strong positions and retreated because their officers had no confidence in the staying powers of battalions to the right or to the left.

Many of those who tried to build up the Republican army have since written books to explain their failure. There is widespread agreement that the Nationalists won because their morale was better, and because the Republican military effort was cramped and hampered by the political control of the Communists. I brought back with me to England a curious collection of pamphlets that I found in trenches captured from the Republicans, among them the notes for a speech delivered in English by a political commissar to an American battalion on the supreme importance of an orthodox interpretation of Dialectical Materialism, and a dreary little pamphlet on the alleged phallic origin of Christianity. "The rod of Moses was clearly a phallic symbol." "Poor devils," said General Fuller; "fancy serving out all this dull stuff! What they want is *La Vie Parisienne*."

Political considerations which hampered the military effort proved even more fatal to the industrial effort. The attempt to eliminate at one fell swoop the "profit motive" resulted not only in widespread inefficiency but also in universal corruption. The demand for a *levée en masse* and the indiscriminate arming of workers had a disastrous effect on production. It is much more amusing to lounge about with a rifle than to do an honest day's work. Thousands of oranges, which would have procured foreign exchange if exported, were left rotting on the quays because the men who should have been loading them found it more amusing to round up and shoot Fascist suspects.

The peasants, who were angered by the persecution of the Church and infuriated by the incompetence of bureaucratic control, lost heart. It was interesting to contrast the carefully cultivated fields in territory that had been under Nationalist control since the outbreak of the war with the ill-kempt disorder and neglect of the territory captured from the Republicans.

I met at Malta, in March 1940, an Italian who had helped to organise the anti-Fascist brigades which fought in Spain on the Republican side. "The principal reason for the Republican defeat," he told me, "was the insensate savagery of the Anarchists. The Spaniards are a cruel race, far more cruel than the Italians. We Italians do not want to kill or to be killed. If we have a revolution in Italy we shall shout a great deal and shoot very little. But in Barcelona they shot a great deal and were very silent. The Spanish Anarchist exaggerates the vices of the Spaniard and has none of his virtues, excepting courage. He has no sense. I used to try to convince these fools that they would lose the war if they continued to burn churches and to murder priests. But they were pure fanatics beyond the reach of reason. The Republic needed the support of the peasants, and lost that support by its campaign against the Church, for the Spanish peasant is, and will always be, a Catholic."

The Republican leaders did not under-estimate the influence of Catholicism or the folly of the religious persecution, but they were impotent to restrain the anarchists and Communists. Very few of their supporters in England realised the decisive importance of the religious issue. English Liberals have always assumed that all foreigners are more interested in politics than in religion, and that the majority of foreigners ask for nothing better than to be governed by the nearest available equivalent to Mr. Gladstone or Mr. Asquith. The English, in general, whatever their political views, find it difficult to believe in the power of ideas which they find uncongenial, and in the existence of popular support for leaders such as Hitler, Mussolini or General Franco, whose views are so painfully un-English.

Progressive opinion in England assumed that Franco would have no friends in Spain except among priests and aristocrats, and that the people would instinctively rally to the support of a government which permitted the active persecution of the religion that was the religion of the overwhelming majority of the Spanish people. Catholicism and Nationalism may be regrettable survivals from a reactionary age, destined to disappear in the enlightened world of to-morrow, but no sound estimate of contemporary Europe is possible if it disregards the immense influence of these ancient loyalties.

ABOUT THE AUTHOR

Arnold Lunn was born in Madras, India on April 18, 1888. He was a student at Harrow, graduated from Balliol College, Oxford in 1911, and received his Ph.D. from the University of Zurich in 1954. In 1952 Lunn was knighted "for his services to British ski-ing and Anglo-Swiss relations."

Sir Arnold originated the slalom and will go down in history as the father of downhill ski racing. He wrote the first Alpine racing rules, basically unchanged to this day, and co-founded with Hannes Schneider the famous Arlberg-Kandahar competition.

He was the author of many books including *The Harrovians* (1913), an exposé of public school life; *Now I See* (1933), published after he had turned from militant atheism to Roman Catholicism, and *Spanish Rehearsal*, his personal account of the Spanish Civil War (1937).

In his long career as ski-mountaineer, lecturer and writer, Arnold Lunn was known for his unfailing good humor, his energy, his faith, and for his actively spirited Christian concern.

He was a brilliant polemicist and engaged in lively controversy from his desk as editor of the *British Ski Year Book*, and his aerie in Mürren, Switzerland where he spent the winters facing out across the Lauterbrunnen valley. In one of his last books he described a traverse of the Bernese Oberland that started before sunrise; he ended with these words: "Only those who have earned the dawn by climbing through the cold night can fully appreciate the benediction of the sun."

Sir Arnold died in London on June 2, 1974.